The Baby Diaries

Tess Daly
The Baby Diaries

Memories, milestones
and misadventures

Vermilion
LONDON

10 9 8 7 6 5 4 3 2 1

Published in 2010 by Vermilion, an imprint of Ebury Publishing

A Random House Group Company

Copyright © Tess Daly 2010
Tess Daly has asserted her right to be identified as the author of this Work
in accordance with the Copyright, Designs and Patents Act 1988

The Random House Group Limited Reg. No. 954009

Addresses for companies within the Random House Group can be found at
www.randomhouse.co.uk

A CIP catalogue record for this book is available from the British Library
The Random House Group Limited supports The Forest Stewardship Council (FSC),
the leading international forest certification organization. All our titles that are
printed on Greenpeace approved FSC certified paper carry the FSC logo. Our paper
procurement policy can be found at www.rbooks.co.uk/environment

Designed by Smith & Gilmour, London
Illustrations by Phoebe Kay, aged five

Picture Credits
Pages: 9, 11, 12, 16, 29, 47, 60, 74, 87, 91, 106, 127, 152, 155, 160, 175, 178, 184, 203, 229, 234,
245, 260, 263, 269, 272, 275, 276, 280: David Venni. Page 99: Getty Images. Pages 45,
72, 199: © BBC. All other photographs are author's own.
Background patterns on cover and throughout taken from *Textile Motifs of India*,
published by The Pepin Press, www.pepinpress.com

Printed and bound in Germany by Firmengrippe Appl, Wemding

ISBN 978 0 09 193516 0

To buy books by your favourite authors and register for offers visit www.rbooks.co.uk

The information in this book has been compiled by way of general guidance in
relation to the specific subjects addressed, but is not a substitute and not to be
relied on for medical, healthcare, pharmaceutical or other professional advice
on specific circumstances and in specific locations. Please consult your GP before
changing, stopping or starting any medical treatment. So far as the author is aware
the information given is correct and up to date as at 2009. Practice, laws and
regulations all change, and the reader should obtain up to date professional advice
on any such issues. The author and publishers disclaim, as far as the law allows, any
liability arising directly or indirectly from the use, or misuse, of the information
contained in this book

To my dad, who would have been so proud of his four gorgeous grandchildren.

To my wonderful mum and my sister Karen, who I hope lets me off for sharing the story about Finn trying to claw his way out of the bedroom.

To my husband, for giving me not one, but two beautiful babies, and, of course, to my girls, Amber and Phoebe.

Contents

Introduction 10

Prologue 14

The First Trimester
Weeks 1 to 13

I'm Pregnant! 18

Preparing for Pregnancy 23

Everything Changes 26

Work in the First Trimester 42

My Childhood 48

The First Scan 58

The Second Trimester
Weeks 14 to 27

Changing Bodies 62

Style in the Second Trimester 65

Exercise 68

Planning for the Big Day 69

Work in the Second Trimester 71

What's in a Name? 73

Discovering I Needed a Caesarean 75

Wanting a Natural Birth the Second Time Around 76

Birth 'Advice' 78

Feeling the Baby Kick for the First Time 82

The Second Scan – Time to Find Out the Sex? 84

The Third Trimester
Weeks 28 to Due Date

Baby Paraphernalia **90**

Buying Clothes for Your Baby **96**

Style in the Third Trimester **98**

Bye Bye Feet **101**

To Wax or Not to Wax? **102**

Grocery Shopping **103**

Decorating the Nursery **105**

Preparing for the Hospital **108**

Aches and Pains **120**

Work in the Third Trimester **122**

Birth Anxiety **123**

The Final Week **125**

Preparing for the Birth **127**

The Births

Phoebe: The Caesarean **130**

Amber: The Natural Birth **137**

Reality Bites

Bringing Our Baby Home **154**

Feeding **162**

New Baby and Sleep **176**

Taking Your Baby Out and About for the First Time **180**

Using a Dummy **184**

Outside Help **187**

Baby Blues **191**

Going Back to Work **196**

Six Months Onwards

I Really am a Mum! 202

Going on Holiday with a Baby 204

Little Personalities 220

Vaccinations 224

Sleep (Or Lack Thereof!) 226

Weaning and Introducing Solid Food 236

Parenting 241

Reading and Playing 244

Style for Little Ones 254

Baby Number Two

Deciding to Have Another Baby 262

So Far with Amber ... 264

Having Two Children 270

Epilogue 274

List of Useful Websites 282

Index 284

Acknowledgements 288

Introduction

The journey from finding out you are pregnant to becoming
a mum for the first time is one of the most exhilarating,
nerve-racking and downright exhausting things we can ever
experience. Of course, everyone seems to have lots of advice
about their own pregnancy and time bringing up babies, but
there are no hard and fast rules for becoming a mum for the
first, second or even third time. And even though I was thrilled
to bits to be given the opportunity to write a book I really didn't
want to make it some finger-wagging 'Thou Must Purée Organic
Food and Be a Supermum' read. I wanted to share my honest
experiences, good and bad, as a working mother. I also wanted
to write a bit about style and fashion during pregnancy and
when you become a mum. Obviously fashion will be way down
your list of priorities when the baby comes. You will have a
beautiful new baby to look after and whether your shoes match
your top may well be the furthest thing from your mind. To
be honest, for the first few weeks after having Phoebe I was
so overwhelmed by this little person and the fact that I was
responsible for looking after her that I was over the moon to
manage to accomplish even the simplest task, such as brushing
my teeth by lunchtime! But I do think that what you wear is
linked to how you feel and just because you are approaching
motherhood doesn't mean you have to put your hair in curlers
and start wearing a housecoat. There may be times when you
think that you'll never be back in your pre-pregnancy skinny
jeans again, but there are lots of ways to adapt your style to
your pregnancy and post-birth shape.

I know that when I first found out I was pregnant I sought out stories of other women's journeys through their pregnancies and subsequent labours. I was looking for reassurance. I wasn't blindly hoping that someone would say, 'Labour? What a doddle!' Or, 'Being a mum for the first time? Nothing to it.' The opposite in fact. I knew that it was going to be a challenge, and I wanted to hear how other women had coped. I wanted to find out whether there were any tricks of the mummy-trade or if it all just trial and error.

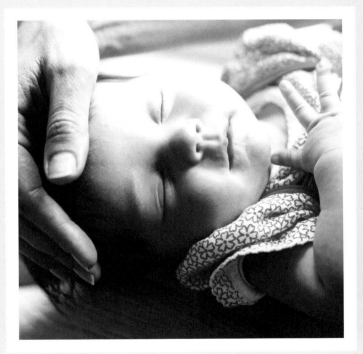

And this didn't just apply to my first pregnancy. Having had a Caesarean section with Phoebe, our first daughter, I was hoping for a natural delivery the second time around. I became obsessed by other women's birth stories. Labour seemed like such an unknown quantity to me. How had other women coped with the pain? What if it was unbearable and I had gone too far to have an epidural, and just had to put up with it? Had other women been as nervous as me? What if my waters broke in the supermarket? What if I didn't know how to push and my baby couldn't come out? What if we didn't get to the hospital in time and I had to give birth in the footwell of the car – or worse still, the car park! I was driving myself mad with endless 'what ifs'!

It was hearing other women's stories that calmed me and came to inspire me – surely if they could push and produce a little miracle I could too? So I hope that in sharing what I have learned as I've become a mum for the first and second time a little of it might be helpful in some way, even if it's only as bedtime reading as you wrestle under the covers trying to accommodate a lump the size of a football where a flat stomach used to be.

So this is my story of me becoming a mum. From standing in the loo waiting for the magical blue line to appear, to sitting here now with my two beautiful daughters, Phoebe who is nearly five, and Amber who is already eight weeks, and wondering how two children can create more mess than the aftermath of a music festival. I hope you enjoy it.

Love Tess
x x

Prologue

Here I am again ... the fourth night of little sleep. My boobs are aching, there are circles under my eyes that an entire tube of Touche Éclat would struggle to fix and I'm so tired I could cry. It's 3 a.m. and, for the third time tonight, I have been awake for the past hour feeding my gorgeous brand-new baby daughter Amber. She isn't sleeping too well at the moment. And it isn't just because she is so small that she has yet to work out the difference between day and night. The poor little mite has been diagnosed with gastric reflux – like heartburn to you or me – that is making her grizzly and she is finding it difficult to settle.

It is also 26°C (78°F). How do I know this? Because I'm sitting staring at the egg-shaped nursery thermometer that tells me so. It offers a smiley face for a room at the correct temperature for a newborn baby and a frowning face for a room that is too warm. At the moment it is positively snarling at me. I've opened the windows, I've put a fan on, but then decided that it cools the room down too much, and I've wafted her with a copy of *Elle*. Are her hands looking a bit blue? Is she too cold now? Should I change her? I nervously wonder. She's wearing a cute little Grobag that claims it's for the summer months, but summer months where? Here? The Gambia? I decide to change her and she snuffles as I put her into a babygro. But then she might be too cold if the temperature drops. Argh! New mum panic has set in yet again. Am I doing things right? Is she positioned correctly in the cot? Does the back of her neck feel too hot? Is it safe for her to sleep on her side? Help! Talk about paranoid. I know that I'm not alone, that there are thousands of other mums out there going through the same thing. But as I sit here on the night shift and Vernon is soundly asleep in the spare room as he has to work early tomorrow, it's easy to feel that I'm the only person looking out of the window feeling on the verge of sleep-deprived temporary insanity.

I thought it might be slightly different this time around. After more than three years of broken sleep with our first daughter, Phoebe, both myself and Vernon had gone into complete denial about the prospect of heading back to a twilight world of walking around like zombies and hoping that one night soon we'd reach the Holy Grail of a full night's unbroken sleep ... at the same time! I grew to envy those mums with their stories of getting their three-month-old babies into a routine and having them sleep through the night. What were we doing wrong? What were they doing right? It made me want to grab them and demand 'How? What's the secret? Tell me how you've done it!'

Throughout my pregnancy with Amber we tried not to think about the sleepless nights we faced. We didn't know how we'd tackle it the second time around; we just knew that going down that dark sleepless route again just wasn't an option. It would be different this time around, we naively convinced ourselves, wouldn't it? Us being experienced parents and all that – water off a duck's back surely. And maybe it will, it really is early days, but at this very moment in time what I wouldn't give for a magic wand that would allow me and my little girl a few hours of peaceful sleep. And if it could magic this room into being the right side of 26°C then that would be just perfect ...

The First Trimester
Weeks 1 to 13

I'm Pregnant!

February 2004

I'm very rarely sick. Once on a working trip to Goa I was the only one of a team of ten who didn't succumb to the dreaded Delhi Belly. So when, completely out of the blue, I ran to the toilet and threw up one day I knew something was definitely afoot. So did Vernon. As I emerged from the toilet we looked at one another and he immediately shot to the shops to buy a pregnancy test. He came back with two. Just to be on the safe side.

I stood in the toilet of our Maida Vale flat, where we lived at the time, doing the pregnancy test dance: look at the stick, nothing's changed, hop from one foot to the other, wave the stick (what did I think waving it would do exactly?), look back at the stick, still nothing, hop from one foot to the other again. I left it on the toilet lid for a couple of minutes and then, after the longest wait of my life, picked it back up again and stared at the result display: one blue line crossing the other blue line. I looked at the instructions: *cross for pregnant, one line for not pregnant*. I looked back at the testing stick again. No, it couldn't be … yes it could, I really was pregnant!

I ran out of the toilet to tell Vernon. After whooping with delight the first thing he said was, 'I've got to tell my mum.' I really wanted to tell my mum too, but what if we'd got it wrong? What if we were the 1 per cent where the test result was incorrect? So of course we did the other test and the blue line began to creep across indicating a positive result; it was looking fairly likely that I was pregnant. We both agreed that we'd better make 100 per cent sure before Vernon ran all the way to Bolton in excitement, so I made an appointment at the doctors and went for a blood test.

At the time I was presenting a Channel 5 programme called *Back to Reality* where a group of reality stars, from Jade Goody to James Hewitt, were brought together in a house and we watched the ensuing fun. The schedule was fairly gruelling, often working 16-hour days (we were even given a mattress in the dressing room so that we could get 40 winks between takes). Before the tell-tale sign of being sick, it hadn't really struck me that I was pregnant, if I'm honest I didn't even know what signs to look for.

One thing that had been happening over the previous few weeks before the pregnancy test was that I'd gone off alcohol. When the cast and crew would gather at the end of a hard day's shooting to unwind with a few drinks I found that I couldn't get past the first one. This wasn't like me. I like to have a few glasses of wine – I'm not Oliver Reed by any stretch of the imagination, but I don't like to just have one dry sherry and then head off for an early night either. It was obviously my body's way of telling me that I needed to look after myself. Not everyone feels like this and a lot of mums beat themselves up about the wild nights they had out before realising they were pregnant.

GPs are fairly reassuring on this matter; the general advice seems to be to try not to worry too much if you've been partying like Paris Hilton – what's done is done – and just start to look after yourself and your baby as soon as you discover that you're pregnant. This is certainly the case during the first trimester when you should drink very little – or none at all. Also, if you are planning to get pregnant it's a good idea to cut right back on your alcohol intake.

So I was in my dressing room the following day wondering if I had time for a little nap when the call came through from the doctors confirming that I was indeed pregnant. After doing a few cartwheels around the room, I quickly rang Vernon and told him. He was over the moon at the prospect of becoming a dad and was now finally allowed to tell his mum. Vernon's mum was so excited that he had to hold the phone away from his ear. 'I've got to phone your Aunty Irene!' She shrieked. As Vernon's mum is one of 13 we knew that it wouldn't just be Aunty Irene who would be receiving a phone call that evening.

My mum was equally delighted at the prospect of becoming a grandmother for the first time. My dad had passed away in September 2003 and it had been such a sad time for us all that the announcement of our pregnancy in February 2004 seemed to give Mum a real boost. There would be a new life in the family and finally something positive for her to focus on.

Around the time I found out that I was pregnant, Vernon began work on a TV show in LA called *The Grill* on Channel 4. I had just finished working on *Back to Reality* and since it would be a few weeks before I would start work on a new show based on an old format for the BBC, which would be called *Strictly Come Dancing*, I decided that my mum and I deserved a holiday. My mum had never been outside the UK, or on a plane for that matter, so when I suggested Miami I think she was initially a little taken aback. It didn't take her long to adjust and she loved it. I think we both really benefited from this holiday. It was a good chance to get away and have some quality time with Mum, but I also knew that my days of a good night sleep and a lie in were numbered and any chance to treat myself had to be taken now. I would definitely recommend that if you get the chance of a break during your pregnancy jump at it! And also if you get the chance to have a lie-in jump at it too, because trust me, once the wee one is here your next guaranteed lie-in is probably, ooh ... 13 years away at least!

The evening after I'd confirmed that I was pregnant, I returned home to our flat and Vernon and I began to discuss what being parents would be like. Practicalities came first. At the time our apartment in Maida Vale was nice but it wasn't exactly family home material. We had a roof terrace that was about the size of a Ford Fiesta and we were three flights up with no lift. Not exactly ideal for a pram! So we started talking about houses in the country. We decided we'd really like to move somewhere a little further afield, but still commutable to London and with a garden. It felt very grown up having a conversation about moving somewhere for our unborn child. Until now, aside from work commitments, we'd been able to do what we pleased when we pleased. It was also a big decision to move back to the countryside after living in big cities all my adult life. It felt like I would somehow be going full circle, but both Vernon and I agreed we were ready for the change. We got on the Internet and started looking at houses, dreaming about where we might live. We knew that it would probably be a while before we'd find exactly what we wanted, but we wanted to make a start.

We also briefly discussed names, but it quickly became clear that we weren't going to readily agree on anything so we left it for that evening. It just seemed so mad that we were going to be parents, but it also gave us a sense of urgency; things had to be done before the baby arrived. I'm sure all expectant mums know that feeling. Everything has to be organized and boxed off before the baby is here but I hadn't realized it would start the moment I found out I was pregnant.

It's such a strange sensation, knowing that you are carrying a little person inside of you and that your life has just changed for ever. I was only five weeks pregnant at the time so it wasn't as if I was showing or that I felt hugely different physically, but I was now suddenly very protective of the tiny life I was responsible for. I would look down at my stomach, imagining a bump there and thinking about the person that the bump would become. What would it feel like being seven, eight and nine months pregnant? Would I have a nice neat bump? Or would my bum help carry the burden and I'd end up looking like I was hiding a rubber ring? It was hard to believe that something inside of me right now, no bigger than a grain of rice, would one day be charging around the house, dressing her dad up as Angelina Ballerina and deciding that sleep was for losers. I wondered who he or she would look like, going through all the Identikit permutations that my and Vernon's physical characteristics would allow. I found all of this hard to imagine, but it was nice daydreaming about it.

Preparing for Pregnancy

It was only three months after our wedding day that I found out I was expecting. I really didn't think that I would get pregnant this quickly, and with good reason. It's funny how many years of our lives most of us spend trying not to get pregnant and having to negotiate the necessary minefield of contraception. The tyranny of the Pill – did I take it this morning? I think so … can't remember. Oh well, better take another one to be on the safe side. Oh great, now my boobs are going to explode because I've overdosed on oestrogen. Condoms – hardly the most attractive of things. The coil – this might be very effective, but anything that can rust inside you is to be approached with extreme caution in my opinion. A cap – can you just hold on two ticks and think sexy thoughts while I pop something in that looks like half a tennis ball? We spend so much of our early adult years avoiding getting pregnant we often just assume that when we decide that it is finally time it will be a doddle. It was only when things became serious between me and Vernon that I started to think about my fertility and decided to address something I'd been avoiding for years.

I hadn't always had irregular periods. But once I got into my early twenties and found myself travelling as much as I did my internal clock went haywire. At the time, I was working as a model and an example of a typical week was to fly from Paris, where I lived, to Germany for a catalogue shoot, then on to Sweden to shoot a feature for Swedish *Elle* and then a long haul flight somewhere in the world for a TV commercial. I often felt that I spent more time in the air than I did on the ground.

Once my periods became irregular I always meant to sort it out, but to be honest – and this may sound like a terrible confession – it felt like a blessing. I had a period on average once every four months and at the time that suited me fine. A lot of the modelling assignments I was given in my twenties were for swimwear and lingerie companies. Turning up with a little period pot belly and having to stand around all day in an ice-white bikini with my fingers crossed wasn't exactly ideal, so the fewer periods I had the better. I didn't think that my topsy-turvy menstrual cycle could be down to anything other than my hectic travel schedule. Admittedly doing nothing at the time probably wasn't the best approach to my gynaecological health, particularly as I later found out that even if you have irregular periods you need to have three or four per year to be safe as otherwise it can increase the risk of womb cancer. But I just pushed it to the back of my mind and told myself that once I stopped travelling things would settle down, and if not I'd deal with it at some stage soon.

Just before we got married I decided that the time had definitely come to address the issue. I booked myself in at the hospital and didn't really know what to expect. Now that I was finally confronting this problem my mind ran riot and I began to worry. Irregular periods could mean anything and I'd been ignoring them for years.

The gynaecologist performed some tests, among them a blood test. When the results came back he told me that I had abnormally high levels of prolactin and it was this that caused my very irregular periods. Prolactin is a hormone that is produced by the pituitary gland. Increased levels of prolactin occur naturally during pregnancy and when we produce breast milk; it also acts as a mild contraceptive, but midwives are at pains to stress that it is not a reliable form of contraception alone.

There are a number of reasons why someone might have high prolactin levels, but for me it was just that I had naturally always had high levels. The consultant informed me that, had this gone unchecked, I would have been unable to conceive. Luckily, however, this is a problem that is treatable and I was prescribed something called Dostinex. I had to take half a tablet a week to lower my prolactin levels. It seemed amazing to me that a little tablet like this could make such a world of difference. So I set about taking it and Vernon and I discussed the fact that it might be a while before we'd hear the pitter-patter of tiny Kays around. How wrong we were!

My mum and her twin sister

Everything Changes

When you become pregnant it is easy to think that your body has a mind of its own. You begin expanding, your appetite goes haywire, your nose is more sensitive than a bloodhound's and your emotions are heightened to the point that you sometimes wonder if you'll ever be sane again. Below I've listed a few of the things that I experienced. You may sail through your pregnancy and not have any side affects whatsoever, but if you are up cleaning at three in the morning or have cried at a picture of a kitten on a china plate in a Sunday supplement recently then you might understand what I'm talking about.

Morning Sickness

Most mums I've talked to didn't have 'morning sickness' – some had all day, every day sickness and some didn't feel at all off colour during their pregnancy, but most described feeling nauseous at some stage in their pregnancy, especially in the first trimester. For the first 12 weeks with Phoebe I felt pretty grotty, but the only time I actually threw up was the catalyst for the pregnancy tests. The rest of the time I had a low-lying, ever-present nausea that wasn't very pleasant! It was explained to me that it's not until you enter your second trimester, when the placenta is fully grown, that the baby has its own system to feed from. Until then all of its nutrients are coming from you, the poor bedraggled mummy. No wonder most women feel awful for the first three months. And then there's the tiredness. It feels a bit like walking through treacle all day long. For those first few weeks with Phoebe the thought of going to bed was the one thing that kept my going.

With Amber I had the added problem of wanting to announce that I was pregnant in my own time. At that point we were on the sixth series of *Strictly* so hiding how dreadful I felt was a challenge. The first I heard about my pregnancy with Amber was when *GMTV* announced it one morning, congratulating myself and Vernon on our good news. I wasn't pregnant! It turned out that the presenter, Richard Arnold had misread an article saying that I *wasn't* pregnant and thought that I was! I got into work that morning and was greeted by Anton du Beke and Brucie who both said, 'Darling, congratulations!' It's one thing being pregnant and having everyone happy for you, but it's a whole other embarrassing thing when everyone thinks that you're pregnant when you're not.

The next day *GMTV* made an announcement saying that they'd got it wrong. I just hoped that this would clear the matter up, although there was no way of guaranteeing that whoever had been watching when my 'pregnancy' had been announced would now be watching to hear that I wasn't. I was sure I was going to be being unduly congratulated for the next nine months.

So when, very shortly afterwards, I began to feel those familiar signs of early pregnancy I initially dismissed it. After a few days, however, curiosity got the better of me and I bought (the obligatory) two tests. This time I didn't wait until I was safely at home. I went straight to the nearest toilets, which happened to be the ones in Marks & Spencer on Kensington High Street, and did my little pregnancy test dance again there. I really wasn't expecting to be pregnant, as I'd had to take

Dostinex again to regulate my prolactin levels, but I should have known from last time that it really is a miracle drug. As the little line came up confirming I was pregnant, I was totally gobsmacked. I had to sit down. Not here though, I thought. So I plonked myself in Wagamama's, ordered a bowl of noodles I couldn't eat, and kept sneaking a look at the pregnancy test in wonder. I couldn't even call Vernon as I was surrounded by fellow diners and knew I wouldn't be able to keep my voice down. So I had the idea of putting the test in a white box with a big ribbon around it and presenting it to Vernon when I got home. At first he couldn't quite make out what he was looking at, his face was a picture of confusion. But the next moment it dawned on him and he was absolutely chuffed to bits. He jumped up, grabbed me and spun me around in delight. I felt like the best Santa ever!

I know that over-the-counter pregnancy tests are accurate and don't need to be confirmed by the doctor – it's really only once you are pregnant that you should pay them a visit – but I did make an appointment with my GP. Once I'd had confirmation from her, my first thought was how happy I was, my second was: Oh no, I've just told everyone I most definitely am not pregnant – it's me with egg on my face now. We decided that we would keep it to ourselves for as long as we could and anyway we wanted the opportunity to reach the 12-week mark when the risk of miscarriage drops dramatically and its safer to tell people.

In November 2008 I presented *Children in Need* with Terry Wogan. It was a great night, we raised a record amount of money and I finally got the opportunity to partner up with Anton du Beke and become one of the *Strictly* girls for one evening only. The only problem was I felt absolutely dreadful. I was about nine weeks pregnant at the time and had come

down with a horrible bought of flu. On screen, thanks to one hot little dress and my brilliant make-up artist Sarah Burrows, I just about got away with it, but underneath the make-up and the frock I was sweating and horribly nauseous. I remember thinking, if I can just make it to the news, I'll be able to sit down or vomit but at least I won't do it on screen. There was a bit at the end of the dance when Anton twirls me around and around. I could hear the crowd cheering as I counted to 20 and tried not to think about throwing up on live TV. I managed to get through the evening and six hours of live TV; I don't think anyone noticed. I got home that night and crept into bed feeling like death warmed up. Then, less than six hours after getting home, I had to head off and do it all again, as it was the *Strictly* live show the following day. I don't mind being green and feeling like death warmed up in the comfort of my own home, but inflicting myself on 10 million viewers twice in two nights in this lurgied state was a bit much! I think the adrenalin and make up saw me through until I could eventually get home and crawl into my sick bed.

Feeling nauseous while pregnant is no fun at all and is even more trying when you already have a three-year-old running round. You can't even treat yourself to an afternoon in bed, not when there's school runs to be done, sandwiches to be made, baths to be had and games to be played. There are lots of old wives' tales of how to tackle sickness in pregnancy, but I think if you find something that works for you then go with it. There doesn't seem to be any tried and tested way to avoid sickness you've just got to live with it as best you can, although if it's really bad and you can't cope your doctor can help. I found that eating little and often eased my nausea. I suppose this isn't rocket science, but it really did help. Having small, manageable meals and snacks meant that I wasn't grabbing for a packet of crisps the size of a horse's nosebag when I was in the supermarket. I had lots of different snacks on hand, fruit, nuts and bread for rounds of toast. Eating this way made me feel as though I was not only staving off morning sickness, but maintaining my energy levels. This way of eating also helped when I was getting towards the end of both pregnancies; carrying a small beach ball sized lump around does give the illusion that you are full all the time. I could manage half a normal-sized meal and feel full only to be hungry again soon after. So learning to pack lots of snacks in my bag meant that I wasn't often caught out.

I also drank ginger tea, having heard that it is a natural cure for nausea and good for the digestive system. But then I read somewhere that in the Far East and India pregnant women believe eating ginger in the first three months of pregnancy can cause miscarriage, since it purifies and thins the blood – as you can imagine I gave up the tea and lived in terror for a while after that. A good source of advice, for such panic station situations is mumsnet.com as it has forums where mums can go on and give advice on what worked for them in all aspects of pregnancy and birth. That way you can try a few of the remedies that other people suggest (apparently peppermint tea is also good for nausea) until you hit on something that works for you.

Mood Swings

The most noticeable change for me with my first pregnancy was that I started to get mood swings. I'd never been a particularly confrontational person, but now that my hormones were all over the place I felt totally erratic. At I mentioned earlier, Vernon was working on the west coast of America for a few weeks for *The Grill* on Channel 4, and with the time change it felt like he was a world away. Even though I managed to go out and see him midway through his time there, once back home I felt quite alone and insecure. I think I just wanted my hubby back and for someone to make me a cup of tea and tell me to put my feet up. I was sad one minute, then deliriously happy the next. When he was back and we had an argument about something and nothing I would throw cushions around the house in unwarranted fits of anger and then feel ridiculous, as I had to pick them back up and rearrange them! I would cry at anything that involved children or small animals on the TV, so the news was out of bounds, as was daytime TV where the RSPCA seem to be big on advertising between *Jeremy Kyle* and *Loose Women*. I also became obsessed by a show called *Birth Stories*. It showed women in labour and giving birth to their babies. Without fail, as soon as that new life came blinking into the world, arms outstretched, emitting its first cry as its little lungs filled with air for the first time, the tears would start to flow. I would sit there in a teary heap on the settee thinking that I couldn't believe this was going to happen to us one day very soon. It was my only guilty pleasure and one that I looked forward to every time it was on.

It is hard to reconcile yourself with being this new irrational person. You can tell yourself that it's hormones all you want, but it doesn't make the feelings any less horrible or real. And it's not just hormones, there is also the psychological effect of the massive changes happening to your life and your body that can affect your mood. I just comforted myself with the knowledge that it would pass and that I'd feel more balanced and like my old self again soon.

Aside from the hormonal mood swings was what I like to call valid mood swings. There was one point when I was pregnant with Amber that I can remember losing it. Okay, I may have been hormonal, but I was also working really hard, not getting much sleep, suffering from evil boomerang flu (it just kept coming back) as well as the small matter of actually being pregnant and I was still having to do the supermarket run and cook tea. Trying hard to curb my cushion throwing, I found that online retail therapy worked as a diversion: Net-a-Porter for those hide-the-credit-card bill splurges and ASOS for day-to-day up-to-date fashion gazing. As well as my beloved *Birth Stories* I also found pure escapism TV, such as *Wife Swap* and *A Place in the Sun,* a great way to relax and calm me down, especially the latter. Will they buy a villa in Puerto Banus, or will they just pretend they like the look of it for the free holiday? Always a good way of taking your mind off being under pregnancy hormone arrest.

Cravings and Aversions

I love my food, but I'm generally pretty healthy and, having been quite the militant vegetarian as a teenager, I still incorporate a lot of vegetarian eating into my diet and steer clear of red meat. However, during my first pregnancy all that I craved was comfort food: fish and chips, mashed potato, stodge, stodge and more stodge basically! Also I developed a real taste for Krispie Kreme doughnuts and would send Vernon out in the dead of night to be the good hunter-gather and bring back a variety pack. I felt that it was my body's way of returning me to my roots and comforting me with food that I had grown up with. You rarely hear of anyone saying, 'I had a real craving for Lollo Rosso lettuce' – it always seems to be good, old-fashioned comfort food that we long for when we're pregnant. With Amber, I again craved comfort food: pain au chocolat or anything chocolate for that matter, Honey Nut Loops and oddly enough Frazzles – having not had red meat for over 20 years craving something bacon-flavoured was a bit weird. Mind you, lots of my girlfriends have reported to going back to meat during pregnancy because they had iron cravings.

As well as being drawn to certain foods I found myself utterly repulsed by some smells. It was as if my sense of smell was on high alert. Cigarette smoke made me physically sick – even the sight of someone smoking in their car was enough for me to pull the car over and dry heave (sorry, but it's true!). I also had to ban Vernon from wearing aftershave, as the smell totally turned my stomach. I felt a bit like one of the Bisto Kids, as if every aroma was something that I could physically see and follow with my nose. As soon as I'd given birth with both of the girls this acute sense of smell disappeared. It really does make you realize how basic and animalistic – in the nicest possible way of course – becoming a mum is. We are programmed to protect our little ones from day one and I find that oddly comforting.

Food and drink

There are a few things that medical experts tell us really should be avoided during pregnancy. Liver, which is fine by me as you couldn't get me to eat liver if you tried. Liver contains a lot of

Vitamin A, which can lead to foetal abnormalities. Pâté of all descriptions can contain listeria, which can lead to miscarriage, so liver pâté butties are obviously to be avoided. Unpasteurized soft cheeses are also a no-no. They can encourage unhealthy bacteria that can be passed to the baby, so steer clear. However, most supermarkets can now point you in the right direction of pasteurised cheese so you don't have to miss out. Shellfish can cause food poisoning so is to be avoided, as is some fish that contain high levels of mercury, which is why I limited myself to a couple of portions of my diet staple tuna a week. Raw eggs can contain salmonella, so it is advisable to make sure that you eat well-cooked eggs and check that any mayonnaise you eat isn't fresh as it contains raw eggs. If you are eating out and are in doubt ask your waiter.

If your caffeine intake is high it is advisable to cut down, although you may have gone off it entirely anyway. Caffeine is a stimulant and any effect that you feel will also be felt by your baby. Health guidelines recommend that pregnant women drink no more than 200mg of caffeine a day, about the same as a one-shot, shop-bought coffee. So you can still have a latte now and again without feeling too guilty. Weirdly, despite never touching the stuff because I'm a good northern tea drinker, I began to crave coffee and would allow myself a vanilla latte as a treat.

Vitamins

If you are trying to get pregnant or are in the early stages of pregnancy it is advised that you take folic acid as this can prevent spinal problems in your baby, such as spina bifida, which can occur before we even know that we're pregnant.

There are lots of vitamin supplements out there that are aimed at pregnant women, but other than folic acid, which we do not produce in large amounts ourselves naturally, a healthy balanced diet should provide you with enough vitamins for you and your baby. Many mums to be do like to take some supplements though, and if you need help most pharmacists will be able to point you in the right direction. Just don't be conned into spending loads of money on something you can get by just eating your dinner. I did feel that sometimes, as new mums, we are a marketing company's dream for all things related to keeping our babies healthy, like buying vitamins that cost a fortune only to find out that they are basically just a bit of fish oil. For me, Pregnacare tablets contained nearly everything I needed and I was also advised by the doctor to take an iron supplement. You should only take extra iron on the advice of your doctor or midwife, who will assess your levels during one of the routine blood tests. Needing to take iron tablets is fairly common during pregnancy, but I must stress that you should only take them if you're told to by a medical professional. I was informed that my iron count had dropped significantly when I had routine blood tests at around 29 weeks.

Napping

One thing I didn't do during either pregnancy, and always meant to, was nap. I know that a lot of mums to be really benefit from having 40 winks in the day, but for me there always seemed to be something else to do, so I never got round to it. I can't say that I regret it, because it's not like you can save sleep up in some sort of sleep piggy bank, but now when I'm feeling sleep deprived in the middle of the night with Amber I wistfully think back to those half hours spent reading through work notes or cleaning the kitchen when I could have been having a snooze. Talking of cleaning the kitchen …

Nesting

I fervently nested. There wasn't one inch of our home that I didn't tackle during both pregnancies. Drawers were pulled out, tidied and streamlined. There wasn't a door handle, skirting board or door top that didn't get wet wiped. I must have gone through a packet a day. Floors were cleaned, clothes were sorted and folded or ones that hadn't been worn for ages were given away. I had a real feeling of out with the old, in with the new and wanted to make sure that our home was ready for our baby. Most women go through this in one form or another and whether it's just a bit of dusting or re-pointing the front of the house, it makes you feel good, as if you are preparing for the arrival of your little one.

I also became germ-phobic about things like public loos – flushing them with my foot and opening the door with my cuff pulled over my hand. Raw meat also set me on edge, convinced that any that had been left lying around for more than a second was contaminated with horrible bacteria.

The Dreaded Booze

The advice varies greatly depending on what you read and who you talk to about consuming alcohol in pregnancy, but most medical professionals advise women to drink less as alcohol

can have a significant and harmful effect on a developing baby. Most women try to abstain as much as possible, but some see a couple of glasses of wine a week as something that helps them through the long nine months. I'm no medical expert so would not assume to offer any advice on this matter, but you get to know your own body pretty quickly during pregnancy and what feels right for you, which hopefully means you're not tempted to be propping up the bar every night at last orders.

As I mentioned earlier, I went off alcohol when I was pregnant with Phoebe and pretty much the same happened again when I was pregnant with Amber. But some women don't. If you are struggling and feel like it will be an eternity until you can next sit down and have a couple of guilt-free glasses of wine then I understand how you feel, but take heart, that day will come. And if you're anything like me, you probably won't feel like it by the time you can drink away to your heart's content. I now find that my capacity for drink is far diminished from my single girl days and I suffer hangovers now that make me think twice about drinking at all! I think it is a combination of getting older and not being built to cope with high kicking nights out and having to get up early and organize the family that make hangovers a thing to be dreaded.

Socializing in Pregnancy

During the first trimester, with both pregnancies, all I wanted to do was stay in and hibernate. It was a combination of feeling pretty rough, really tired and knowing instinctively that I needed to be home and near my fridge and bed. But as I began to regain my energy I really wanted to get back out and about again.

Most of us don't have groups of teetotal friends so our social lives traditionally revolve around eating and drinking with the odd being-good-and-going-to-the-cinema night. Socializing when you are the only sober person in the room can be a bit tricky at first, but soon becomes second nature. When I was pregnant with Phoebe we went out quite a lot. By the time I was about 14 weeks pregnant I suddenly got the fear that I might not have the opportunity to do this again for at least 16 years, by which time I'd be an embarrassing mum. So we got out and about as much as possible.

We even went on a long weekend to Ibiza, where Vernon was DJing, and I took my bump dancing at Pacha. I sipped my pineapple juice as everyone around me got stuck into the margaritas and had a great time. And instead of staying in bed the next morning I was up with the larks enjoying the island.

Being pregnant in social situations can be quite funny, especially around people who are up for a good night out. I noticed that with people I hadn't seen socially for a while. The night could often be predictably divided into three. 1: The beginning of the evening – people are wary of you, you get treated with suspicion at first, like you're the sober enemy in the camp. 2: The night gets going – everyone begins to warm up and speak to you, but cannot seem to talk about anything other than babies as they think that that's all you're interested in. When, sensing their discomfort, you try to veer off the topic of breastfeeding and stitches they breathe a sigh of relief and you too can relax and enjoy yourself. 3: The night tips over into debauchery – everyone seems to get paralytically drunk at the same time, forgets that you're not drinking and tells you their deepest, darkest secrets. You go home and wake up the next morning fresh as a daisy; they go home, wake up and probably think they should have stuck with their first instincts – you were sober, an enemy in the camp and now you are the keeper of all their secrets.

But whatever your nights consist of I believe that going out is good for the soul. So get your glad rags on and some high(ish) heels and go out and enjoy yourself. But don't worry if you don't feel like it. There's always someone ready to tell you that life ends when you have a child and you'll never seen the inside of a club or restaurant again, but that is rubbish in my experience. Life changes, you have to organize yourself more and you won't be out every night of the week, but there's no reason once the babies are here that you can't still have the odd night out and let your hair down. The biggest difference will be that you'll have a lovely baby to come home to.

Work in the First Trimester

After I returned from my holiday to Miami with my mum I was due to begin work on *Strictly Come Dancing*. It was March 2004, the BBC were very excited about their new flagship programme and I was equally excited to be hosting a primetime show alongside Bruce Forsyth, someone I'd watched and loved since I was a child. The BBC had high hopes for the show that was to be based on the old *Come Dancing* format, but would now have a glossy makeover that would incorporate celebrities who may not be particularly known for their dancing skills. Even though there was great belief in the show there was always the chance that it wouldn't work. The viewing figures for the time we aired were largely made up of families and nobody knew if ballroom dance could ignite the imagination of the nation. The show was to air in May 2004, and we would have an eight-week run with no guarantee of a second series.

I went along to the first meeting with Bruce, nervously excited. I was apprehensive about meeting this TV legend, after all he'd been in show business for six decades and hadn't had many female co-hosts, only dollies doing their dealing, but I needn't have worried. Brucie is an absolute gentleman, he was kind and courteous to me from day one and I loved him to bits after the first five minutes. He really is brilliant to work with, a total hoot, full of showbiz stories and an absolute love. He's also very generous and will always share his chocolate wafers, but he draws the line at his precious digestives. Don't try to come between that man and his digestives. He'll chuckle at this because he knows it's true!

I wanted more than anything to prove myself and to show everyone working on the programme that I was up to the job of jointly carrying this new show. I also felt I had to prove to everyone that I was more than capable of doing the job as a pregnant woman. It seems awful to admit in this day and age that we women feel this way, but we do. We have to prove ourselves time and again in the workplace, and I say this knowing that throughout my time on *Strictly* I have been fully supported by my colleagues and the BBC to the extent that they welcomed me back halfway through series two after I'd had Phoebe. To change presenters in this way was fairly unprecedented and I was, and am, grateful for the loyalty shown to me. The pressure to perform was definitely being exerted by me. No one else seemed to feel that being pregnant would hinder my capabilities as a presenter of a live show.

We had six weeks of preparation before the live shows began. I was fitted for my dresses, which were mostly floaty, empire line numbers to cleverly conceal a growing bump – after all TV really does makes you look bigger. I wasn't to be so lucky for series six and pregnancy number two. We had decided before I knew I was pregnant to go for a real 'Body Con' look with bandage dresses galore. This meant that by the time we were nearing the final and I was nearing four months of pregnancy (and we still hadn't told anyone) I was wearing a number of reinforced pants to keep my tummy in check. It was only on the show that aired on Christmas Day – when I thought that I couldn't put another pair of Spanx on without squashing my poor unborn child – that I begged the stylist, the lovely Annabel Kerman, to put me in a floaty dress that under the studio lights clung to my bump. I thought that with a floaty dress I'd at least be able to relax and let it all hang out. How wrong was I? I've never been so relieved, but there was no concealing it, that was a baby bump in all its glory. After managing to keep it so quiet I received an absolute barrage of texts that evening, mostly simply saying, 'Daly, are you pregnant?!' Pregnancy number two was suddenly out of the bag.

When I became pregnant with both girls it was important for me to focus on work. I knew, or at least *hoped*, that when I had my baby I would do everything possible to maintain my career *and* be the best mum I could. I knew there would be a lot of compromises and sacrifices, but that was part and parcel of being a parent.

I'm not daft, and I know that I'm in quite a privileged position. My working life is far from nine-to-five, but working long and late hours on the days that we film brings with it its own challenges. Having worked and been financially independent from the age of 18 I felt that my career partly defined me. I don't mean this in some ladder climbing, *Dynasty*-shoulder-padded way. I just loved my job, I had worked hard to get to where I was and wanted to maintain it now that I was pregnant and about to be a mum.

Speaking to other mums, this is a dilemma that many women face. We spend our twenties and early thirties building up our careers, and just when things are getting to where we dreamed they would be, we start a family. At this early stage in my pregnancy I was trying to keep an open mind as to how I would feel once the baby came along. But I had a sneaking suspicion that I would want to get back to work when I was up to it. Not working never seemed like an option to me. There was no trust fund or silver spoons in our family to fall back on and anyway I loved my job. There was also the worry that if I gave up work I might never be able to pick up where I left off and I might resent the fact that my working life had evaporated. It is such a dilemma; I didn't want to spend precious time away from my baby, but I didn't want to give up work – I wanted to have my cake and eat it. Since then I've discovered that every working mother suffers in this way. No one wants to leave their baby, yet in part their job defines them and they need their work to help them be a better all-round mum.

That said, Vernon and I are quite lucky in that, on the whole, when he is working I'm not and vice versa, although we have orchestrated it that way rather than landing happily on our feet. For example, when Phoebe was two Vernon gave up his Sunday morning Radio 1 show, which he loved doing, so that he could spend more time with the family. I'm very grateful that we've both been able to work this way, although it does sometimes mean sacrifices and we have tried to manage with as little outside help as possible.

My Childhood

As my belly began to expand and I got to know my bump
a little better I really began to think about and appreciate my
own childhood and family life. I grew up in a small village in
Derbyshire, in a two-bedroom terraced house that was still
the family home when I left aged 19. The bedroom that I shared
with my sister Karen looked out on the patchwork hills of the
Peak District. We even slept in bunk beds until I left home. Over
the years, the room transformed from a little girl's room to a
shrine to Duran Duran (me) and the Smiths (Karen). When Karen
was out I would perform a land-grab, sneak her posters down,
put some of mine up and sit back and see how long it took her
to notice that Simon le Bon was pouting down at her. When
I was out she would sneak her posters across onto my side of
the room, so I had Morrissey and his gladioli to contend with
when I got home. When, years later, I was chosen to appear in
not one, but two, Duran Duran videos – 'Serious' and 'Violence
of Summer' – you can only imagine my excitement. It was as
if all those years of loyally displaying my posters had paid off.

Life in the Daly household was fun, busy, loving and on the
whole idyllic. We went shopping to Stockport on Saturday where
Karen and I would rifle through the racks of Tammy Girl, Chelsea
Girl, Clock House, Marks & Spencer and Top Shop, looking for a
bat-winged jumper or some imitation Farrahs. Shopping on
Saturday was such a treat. I never remember having much
pocket money, but I always managed to find something super-
stylish – or at least I thought so at the time, even if it was just a
pair of fluorescent leg warmers, fingerless gloves and a snood.

Every Sunday, without fail, we would have a full Sunday roast with all the trimmings. Dad would carve the meat and mash the potatoes and mum would always get flustered, wiping the steam from her glasses as she tried to get the timings right on the veg. We would all sit down to eat together and talk about what we'd been up to that week. I loved those Sundays.

We had pet rabbits: Binky One, Binky Two and Binky Three. Our thinking must have obviously been that we'd hit on the king of rabbit names and there was no point in deviating from the gold standard. All three Binkies were eventually buried in the top garden with full rabbit funeral honours. My dad would make a wooden cross for whichever Binky it happened to be and we would solemnly bury the beloved pet and say a little prayer for it. I could never bring myself to tread on the ground where we had made our very own pet cemetery, it seemed disrespectful to the dearly departed souls of the Binkies.

Every year we would holiday on the Isle of Wight. It was an eight-hour journey and then a ferry ride to get there, with all of us squashed in the car and the suitcases strapped to the roof. I dread to think how many times me and Karen asked Mum and Dad, 'Are we nearly there yet?' But we loved our annual holiday.

The only really traumatic thing that happened to me as a child was being chased by a flasher with his bits hanging out when I was about 11. The trauma of this was nothing compared to telling the police what had happened and having to say 'willy' in front of my dad. The sheer mortification! Thinking about it now, there always seemed to be a flasher around when we were kids. 'There's a flasher up in the park,' kids would warn one another or, 'There's a flasher on the rec.' Flashing seemed to be a pastime quite particular to the late seventies and eighties.

My mum on her hols – what a babe!

Mum and Dad get married

Karen and I are three and a half years apart in age, and had a typical sisterly relationship: fighting one minute, sticking up for one another and forming a united front against Mum and Dad the next. When I was younger I never really thought about the family that I would have when I was older, I just *knew* – in that young, confident way that you do – that I would have one. I didn't think about the heartbreak of infertility or life not presenting me with the opportunities to have a family of my own, I just assumed that I would have one because that's what people did.

Family for me was just a normal part of life and as an ambitious 'world is my oyster' teenager I was more interested in getting my GCSEs and A' levels then heading out into the world to see what it had to offer, than thinking up baby names and settling down. One day, when I was a sixth former, I was in Manchester city centre with my friend. As she was buying a McDonalds, I was making a vegetarian stance and waiting outside with my arms folded indignantly. It was here that I was approached by a model scout who gave me a flyer and told me to call him. At the time I was quite shy and didn't think I looked anything like a model, so I stuffed the flyer in my pocket and thought no more about it.

A few weeks later, on a Friday afternoon, I was in school and we had an afternoon of no lessons. While rummaging in my pocket I found the flyer again. Without telling anyone I decided to catch the bus into town and head to the model agency to see if they'd been joking and Jeremy Beadle was waiting to pop out of a bin when I arrived. To my surprise they took me on there and then. I didn't know what to think, I was meant to be doing my A' levels, but here was some agent asking me to go to Japan on my first modelling assignment. A bit of me thought, oh the glamour, a lot of me thought, my mum and dad are going to freak. I wasn't far wrong – they weren't exactly ecstatic. They tried to reason with me, to think about what I'd be giving up to go to Japan, how I'd feel living so far away from home and to point out that there were a lot of people out there ready to exploit young models, but I wasn't having any of it. I thought Japan was going to be glamour on a stick.

No wonder Mum and Dad were reticent. If Amber or Phoebe said they wanted to jet off to Japan to work at the tender age of 17, I think Vernon would lock them in a cupboard! Japan was a million miles, geographically and culturally, from where I'd grown up, but I begged them and begged them to let me go until eventually, probably fed up with the earache, they gave in and allowed me to go. So it was in Japan that I was about to get my first taste of the crazy world of modelling.

I had some notion in my head that models flew around the world first class, sipping champagne and generally living the high life. When I got to the airport I quickly realized there wasn't going to be any first-class travel for me, and once I finally saw where I was staying in Japan I realized that I had been lucky they hadn't tried to put me through as hold luggage. The high life it wasn't: the apartment was minute, I had next to no money, I didn't know a single word of Japanese and couldn't make sense of any of the signs. In the end I would get on the bullet train, set the alarm on my watch for the time I guessed I would arrive at my destination and hope that the precision that they were famed for was true; it worked, miraculously.

The whole place was alien to me at first and I felt totally homesick and alone; pretty much as Mum and Dad had predicted. There was no way I was admitting that to them in our weekly conversations, however. I would tell them how glamorous life was in Japan, about how I was trying all sorts of wonderful new things. Looking back, living in Japan was an amazing experience and in my two months there I made some good friends and learned a lot about myself. One of those lessons was that my family were very important to me.

Over the next few years my modelling career took me to a number of glamorous cities. Although the cities may

Me, age three

have been glamorous, but, to begin with, life as a jobbing model was far from it. At least I was beginning to know a few of the other girls from my agency with whom I could share digs. I was paid very little, but I was getting to see the world in a way that no one else I knew was and I felt very lucky. Living in Paris in my early twenties was a turning point for me. Things somehow seemed to fall into place here. I began to earn regular money, the city was beautiful and my confidence – in myself and my ability to survive away from home – was growing.

As time went by I began to get more assignments and to be asked back by people I had worked with before. By the time I was 23 and living in New York things were good, I was getting regular work and making a life for myself there. I lived in New York for the next five years, but at the back of my mind I never really felt that it would be my home. I made great friends and had all the beginnings of a life there: a flat, a bike, even a boyfriend, but I knew that my heart belonged in the UK.

At around this time I had been modelling for over ten years and knew that I needed to think about my future. Models have a short shelf life and, although I was still young, I knew I should start thinking about this now. I promised myself that I'd get out of the industry before it kicked me out. So I began to turn my attentions to a prospective career as a TV presenter and even though I didn't really know what the future would hold, I kind of thought that I would probably end up heading home sometime soon.

I first met Vernon in 1999 on a TV show called *Phone Zone* for the channel UK: Play. I was a roving reporter and Vernon was a studio presenter. On the day we met Vernon offered to film a sketch with me where I was dressed as Britney and he was dressed as Geri Halliwell – I suppose it's one way to meet your future husband! He was funny and we got on brilliantly – not that I was about to tell him I thought he was great. That night I was due to attend a BBC party. When I got there the only person in the room I recognized (and who was standing out a mile as he towered over everyone) was Vernon. I made a beeline for him and we chatted all night. The rest, you could say, is history.

Now, as gorgeous and as much of a laugh as Vernon is, and as much of a brilliant husband and father as he has turned out to be, he didn't immediately strike me as settling-down material. He still had *Maxim* posters on his wall, sprayed Febreze on his laundry instead of washing it, and the only thing in his wallet other than mothballs was a Solo card. He was more like a student than a suave, ex-model, TV presenter. This didn't stop things between us progressing quickly, however. I've never exactly been the type of girl who needs a man to be earning a certain amount of money and driving a fancy car before I'd go out with him; I follow my heart. And thank God for that because things for me could have been a whole lot different if I'd knocked Vernon back for not having a Switch card.

My life at the time was split between New York and the UK, but slowly I began to bring my belongings back to the UK as things between Vernon and I became more serious, until my flat in New York was bare and I had to admit to myself that I was going to be staying here and that most of the reason for my gradual move was Vernon.

One thing I did realize about Vernon, as we got to know each other better, was that he was the first man I'd been out with who I could imagine having children with. I don't mean this in a bunny-boiler way. I wasn't about to insist we leap into family life after knowing each other a few months, we wanted to enjoy ourselves, but it just felt right that one day we would get married and have a family. We had very similar upbringings and similar views on the world, and it felt good to have met someone that I loved and I knew my mum and dad loved too.

Vernon proposed to me on Christmas Day 2002. Both our families were present and everyone had opened their gifts. I remember thinking: where's my present from Vernon? Then, when out of the blue he presented me with the box and went down on one knee, I realized that my present was last because it was pretty special. I think I went bright pink, filled up with tears, squealed with delight and of course said yes. We set the date for September 2003 and married near Vernon's home town of Bolton, the wedding was the most amazing day. Three hundred and fifty of our nearest and dearest came and what made it all the more special was that my dad was there to give me away.

My wonderful dad, the man by which I judge all others, passed away only 18 days after Vernon and I got married. We were still on honeymoon when I found out. I was so dazed with grief that I can't really remember the awful journey home. I was at least comforted by the fact that he got to walk me down the aisle. We knew he was very sick and as his health worsened he'd consistently promised that he would be there at our wedding, no matter what. Sheer determination of spirit meant that he made it – he was always a man of his word, my dad.

My dad and his girls

The First Scan

Most NHS scans take place around the 12-week mark. The
purpose of this scan is to date the pregnancy by measuring
the baby, and it also offers a chance, in combination with blood
tests, to measure an area on the back of the baby's neck to give
a risk of certain conditions like Down's Syndrome or a group
of conditions called neural tube defects, spina bifida is one of
these. Women are given verbal and written information so they
can decide whether to have the screening test. And of course,
it's your first chance to meet your baby!

Most women calculate their due date from the date of their
last period. There are tools to do this on the Internet. Most of
these calculators assume that your cycle is the normal 28-day
cycle. But if, like me you, weren't regular then you can find
calculators that allow you to alter your cycle manually and give
you a more accurate date. However, the measurements given
at the dating scan are the most accurate indication of due
date. This scan also makes sure that a heartbeat is detected
and that the baby's growth is progressing normally.

We couldn't wait for the 12-week mark with my first
pregnancy and so paid for a scan at eight weeks. I had the
initial panic that I'm sure lots of women have: 'Is there really
something in there? I haven't made it up, have I?' But as the
doctor performing the scan ran the scary-looking, hand blender-
type device over my belly and the image of our little peanut-
shaped baby popped up on the screen I felt totally overwhelmed.
I just wanted everything to be okay for her (not that we knew
it was a girl at the time, obviously). I felt for the first time that

I was allowed to be emotional about this little life because it suddenly felt so real. I looked at Vernon and he had tears in his eyes. As I'm writing this I've just asked him if he remembered how it felt when we first saw Phoebe on the scan. 'It felt absolutely brilliant.' He says. And I have to agree, it *did* feel absolutely brilliant, and scary, and pretty surreal to be completely honest – a little heart beat signifying a whole new life. One that would be wholly dependant on, well . . . ME!

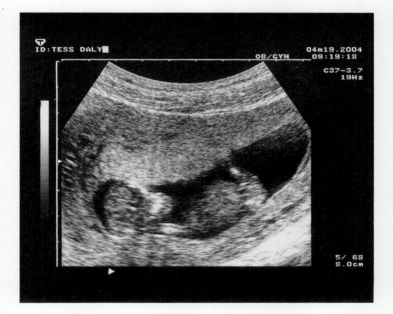

The Second Trimester
Weeks 14 to 27

Changing Bodies

Lots of women understandably struggle with their bodies
changing dramatically during this time – particularly if we've
spent most of our adult life trying to keep trim and in shape.
To suddenly be presented with the fact that all that is about
to change, and that we can't say for certain how we will look
during and after our pregnancy, can be daunting. There is an
assumption that when pregnant we accept readily what is
happening to our bodies. This may be true to a large extent,
as there is little we can do about the way in which we carry
weight during pregnancy, but that doesn't stop the natural
concerns that most of us have. A lot of our identity is wrapped
up in how we look, so having a few concerns about what will
happen physically is perfectly normal.

　　I've always been quite slim, so finding my body changing
was a real wonder to me. I hoped for a nice neat bump, so that
people would know that I was pregnant rather thinking I'd
discovered a penchant for pies. Any concerns I had were dispelled
when my new hips, boobs and bum began to rapidly develop.
Suddenly I had Jessica Rabbit curves (or at least I thought I did!)
and felt really shapely and womanly. I would lie in the bath
marvelling at my new figure and wondering if there was a way
to keep the curves in the right places once the baby was born.

Stretch Marks and Veins

When we are pregnant our bodies become prone to all sorts of
maladies that have never befallen us before. I've spoken to mums

who had warts, mouth ulcers, rashes, eczema and even hair loss during pregnancy. I am very lucky as I didn't get stretch marks with either of my pregnancies, but that's not to say that I didn't live in fear of them mysteriously appearing when I awoke one morning. During my first pregnancy I would slather Bio Oil all over my bump and scan my skin for the dreaded purple marks. Even though I couldn't see any I was convinced that the little silvery tell-tale signs of stretch marks would somehow appear after the baby was born, so I continued with my nightly massage

routine. Towards the end of my pregnancy a midwife told me that stretch marks happen when the skin stretches very quickly and can even run in families, so if your mum didn't have them, then chances are you won't have them either. But I still think it does no harm to massage oil or cream in every night. The soothing circular motion acts as a mini massage for you and is a nice way to connect with your baby bump.

I did, however, discover veins that I didn't know I had. With my first pregnancy they were thin thread veins. They weren't particularly alarming and they did disappear as soon as Phoebe was born. With my second pregnancy though, I got the biggest varicose vein in the world, or at least I thought it was. It was an enlarged vein, blue-coloured and raised, and felt like an alien growing and pulsating on the back of my thigh or some evil latent twin from a Stephen King novel. I dreaded wearing skirts above my knee in case it poked out and scared passersby. I even tried to conceal it with make-up, but it still managed to rear its ugly, alien head . In the end I just had to accept that it was part and parcel of being pregnant (even though it made me cringe to even think about it lurking around) and miraculously almost as soon as I gave birth to Amber, it disappeared. It was as if the pressure on my legs had been immediately alleviated. Thankfully!

Style in the Second Trimester

Around about this time I started looking out for pregnancy clothes as my jeans were beginning to feel tight and some of my tops were beginning to pull a little. I didn't look obviously pregnant with either pregnancy until about week 17, but I knew that I was expanding and I wanted to make sure that we'd moved on from the polyester smocks that my mum's generation had to wear. When I was pregnant with Phoebe five years ago the choice of maternity wear wasn't brilliant, but this time around with Amber, it had vastly improved. Most high-street stores have their own maternity section. It may just be me, but did you always find yourself accidentally in the maternity section when you weren't pregnant and now you are you can never find it? Anyway, if you do manage to find them H&M, Top Shop, Dorothy Perkins, Miss Selfridges, Next, Gap and Zara all have good maternity ranges. As do dedicated baby stores such as Mamas & Papas and Mothercare. Online, ASOS have a maternity section and Mama la Mode has a good selection, but they're generally more pricey, one-off, I've-got-to-go-to-a-wedding-and-I've-got-a-massive-bump purchases. Formes is also good for work wear and formal wear; it is more expensive than the high-street brands, but the fit and cut is excellent for a burgeoning belly. As a general rule maternity tops are longer at the front than the back so they grow with you and don't ride up over your bump. What I tended to do most of the time for my day-to-day wear was to just buy a size or two bigger than usual in floaty dresses and three-quarter length tops and wear them with leggings or jeans. Top Shop do great maternity jeans. The elasticated bit of the jeans sits on the hips instead of being a big belly warming piece of elastic that stretches up to your nipples (the more traditional form that maternity jeans used to take – not very attractive!) and you can get them in skinny and boyfriend cut as well as just normal or boot cut. A couple of good pair of jeans will see you through right up until your due date. Although you might decide that for the last few weeks there's nothing else for it and you have to live in leggings or a comfy tracksuit.

As I felt that what I could wear was more limited than it had been before I was pregnant I began to accessorize – heavily! A good chunky statement necklace and loads of bangles lifted any outfit I was wearing and it's a good way of varying your look without spending loads on clothes that you will only need for a limited period of time.

Bra Buying

I wasn't particularly brilliant at buying new bras when I was first pregnant. You are meant to wear bras without an underwire to allow your breasts to 'develop properly'. Supportive ones like sports bras are meant to be good, but I was at first reluctant to give up my pretty Victoria's Secrets bras for something that looked like a training bra. I was soon to discover, however, that help is at hand. Marks & Spencer do an excellent bra-fitting service and they have a good selection of nice non-wired bras, but be warned, you have to book on the day and if they are busy you might be asked to come back in a few hours, so thinking you can pop in on your lunch break might not be the best idea. Also, I found out that Elle McPherson did a great collection for mums-to-be and they are far from the Cross Your Heart numbers I had imagined I might be forced to wear. Breasts often grow very quickly in the first trimester, settle down in the second and grow again in the third, so do have regular fittings especially if your bras start to feel a little uncomfortable!

Shoes

I love shoes! There's nothing better than slipping on a pair of six-inch-heels and a bit of lip gloss to make a girl feel instantly glam. So now I was pregnant I wasn't about to slip off quietly into the world of orthopaedic shoes without a fight. However, some things have to give when your centre of gravity is shifting daily and the size of my heels had to come down over the course of my pregnancies, which is what medical professionals advise any way. That's not to say I didn't still wear a heel when I went out, but a good pair of ballet pumps or Havaianas in your handbag is the key. You might not need them, but they're like a comfy insurance policy and you can slip them on when your feet begin to ache.

During the day I was far more sensible, wearing ballet pumps, flat sandals and my trusty Converse. I did find my legs ached more than usual if I spent a lot of time standing up or walking, but long soaks in the bath (not too hot!) were a great remedy.

Exercise

I've never been much of a gym bunny – too much sweat and bad cycling shorts for my liking – but I have had a trainer in the past, and I don't rule out the fact that I might find myself back there one day soon, on a treadmill, feeling sorry for myself. I prefer my exercise to be more sedate. The exercise I really like is yoga and swimming. I find both activities relaxing and good for core strength. If you've never tried yoga before it can look a little sedentary, but it really is great exercise. Also there are loads of classes that are now tailored specifically for pregnant women. This involves a lot more concentration on breathing techniques than traditional yoga. And they do usually have a quiet wind-down period at the end of the session for about 20 minutes. Perfect for a little snooze. These classes are geared towards thinking about labour and how – if everything goes smoothly and you have a natural delivery – you can help yourself with breathing techniques, especially during the early stages of labour pains. It wouldn't have worked for me in the later stages of labour with Amber, although I love yoga I was fairly sure that no amount of regulating my breathing and putting myself in a 'happy place' would have helped. An epidural was the only thing that was going to take the edge off that!

Lots of mums-to-be maintain a healthy exercise routine right up until they go into labour. Swimming and walking are both great to see you through pregnancy. It's just probably time to give the spin classes a wide berth for a while.

Planning for the Big Day

Everyone is different and you may feel you need to try and plan for your baby's birth as much as possible. There is plenty of help out there. The National Childcare Trust (NCT) runs courses preparing for childbirth. These groups often prove invaluable in creating a network after the birth where mums can catch up and swap tips or just weep over a cup of coffee about the sleep they once enjoyed. Be warned though, these courses book up early in a lot of areas, it's as if some people are so organized that they manage to book them before they even know they're pregnant! The NHS runs its own Preparation for Birth classes that are free, but they vary from trust to trust and hospital to hospital so ask your midwife how you can access advice and help. These classes will go through everything from coping with early labour to knowing when to go to hospital and what to expect when you get there. The NHS also runs breastfeeding classes that can be booked at the same time as the Preparation for Birth classes.

I didn't really fancy going along to classes with Vernon, I wanted to read up on everything in my own time and digest the information at my own pace. So I read everything I could find about becoming and being a mum. There are so many books and websites out there that I got a bit bogged down for a while and thought that everyone's experience was so different that I really couldn't ever know what to expect, and as such, I might as well just let whatever was to happen, happen. Once I'd got over my mini-panic, however, I went back to the books and realized that, although everyone's stories are different, there is real comfort in knowing that everyone has to go through roughly the same thing. They have to carry the baby and then give birth to it when the time comes. I became quite preoccupied with other people's stories. I wanted all the details and I didn't want to be spared any of the gore.

I will come to the birth of my girls later and I will try to be as truthful as possible. Right now, if you are working and finding it difficult to set aside time to read and research the process of pregnancy and birth don't be too hard on yourself, there are so many books and websites out there that it's easy to think you should be reading all of them. Obviously, if you have time to gen up then great, but do not stress yourself unduly if not. Ultimately on the day you will be surrounded by medical professionals who have done this time and again and you, unless you are having a Caesarean, will know what to do. Just try to look after yourself while you have chance and try not to get too bogged down in constructing a neatly written, ten-page birth plan.

Work in the Second Trimester

Around this time I suddenly got my energy back and felt a
bit more like myself again. This was just as well as with my first
pregnancy I was about to start work on *Strictly Come Dancing*
and the gruelling schedule wouldn't have allowed for a
hibernating mum-to-be. I'm a naturally energetic person and
find it hard to relax, so these first three months of feeling tired
was strange for me and I was glad to be feeling back to
something like normal again.

Being part of a new series is always exciting, but there was
a particular buzz about *Strictly* right from the off that made it
a great place to be. By the time I was into my second trimester
all of the meetings had taken place and I had been introduced
to the dancers and the celebrities. Bruce and I were getting
along really well and we all felt that the pairing would work
well on screen, and the first murmurings and previews in the
press were promising. None of us, of course, had any idea what
a phenomena the show would turn out to be. At that moment
in time it was something that I was really pleased to be part of
and I was going to give it my all. I knew that once I had finished
the show I would be seven months pregnant and that bit closer
to meeting my baby. I was still convinced I was having a girl, but
had nothing other than my own based-on-nothing hunch that
this was the case.

David Dickenson was a contestant on that first series and
during one episode his wife Lorne had come to cheer him on.

When she saw me backstage she came flying over to me, took one look at me and said, 'It's a girl'. She then went onto describe my baby as having blond hair, blue eyes and one ear that bent over slightly. I swear that woman really is a baby psychic. That is exactly what Phoebe looked like when she was born and it still describes her today.

It was great fun working on this new, frenetic live show. And those eight weeks flew by. I love being really busy and for me it was important to be working hard during both pregnancies, as I could easily have become preoccupied and obsessive about becoming a mum. It will be really nice in the future to sit down with the girls and have the unique opportunity to show them what their mummy was doing when they were in my tummy. Not that I'm sat at home watching re-runs of myself!

What's in a Name?

It is so tough choosing a name for your baby, but it's something you can't help thinking about right from the word go. To know that the name you give your little one is something that they will be blessed with – or stuck with – for their entire life can make the choosing an onerous task. Everyone has a story of a Richard Head or a Tom Bowler (Vernon's best mate is called Luke Downes!), so we were careful early on to be mindful to avoid such pitfalls. Some people have traditional family names to draw on and Vernon quite liked the idea of incorporating our mother's maiden names into a boy's name, Bradley or Taylor. Although I much preferred more modern names to traditional ones, this wasn't an idea I was opposed to, the only problem here was that I was adamant we were having a girl.

We bought a baby name book and began searching through it, imaging our new baby (girl, obviously) and whether certain names would suit her. Some of the names had us creased with laughter, but I won't say which ones as no doubt they are someone else's idea of the perfect name. One name that we did go back to however was Phoebe. It was a name that we both liked and somehow felt right. It means the Shining One in Greek, which I thought was perfect. One night we were watching a film where the heroine was called Phoebe, I'd love to say it was a landmark film – like when people call their little girl Scarlett because of *Gone with the Wind* – but I can't even remember what it was about! Yet it somehow cemented the idea that this was the right name for us, 'If we have a girl,' Vernon reminded me. *When* we have a girl, I thought.

When it came to naming Amber we went back to the same boys' names, but this time for a girl I liked Liberty, Arabella and Kitty. Vernon quite liked Kitty but couldn't get to grips with Arabella because he'd had a cat called Bella as a child. Years ago I had met the supermodel Amber Valetta. She had been so sweet, and by far the nicest of the supers, that the name had stuck with me. I mooted it with Vern and he pulled a face that suggested that he was allowing it to bed in and then nodded his approval. He liked Amber, he said, and so Amber went to the top of our list of names for our second baby.

Discovering I Needed a Caesarean

Around this time in my pregnancy with Phoebe I was told that I would need a Caesarean. Some abnormal cells had shown up. They were something that were treatable, but only after I had had my baby. I sought three different doctor's opinions, desperate to be allowed the chance of a natural birth, but all said the same thing. I had to resign myself to the fact that it wasn't going to happen. I was really sad about this, but knew that all the doctors wanted was to produce a healthy mother and baby and that I shouldn't feel a failure in any way. How would I feel, I wondered, when they handed me the baby that I hadn't had to push for, but had just been pulled from me after being gowned up and taken into theatre? I tried not to get too upset about it and to look at the positives: I was on track to have a healthy baby and they were advising a Caesarean for good reason.

Also with a Caesarean I knew the date that my baby would be born and I could read up about what a Caesarean entailed. There didn't seem to be such a fear of the unknown as there is with natural childbirth. That didn't mean to say it was something that I preferred. I just had to accept it and plan towards my operation date – in something as uncertain as childbirth a date and an operation time seemed to offer a little bit of certainty.

Wanting a Natural Birth Second Time Around

When I discovered that I was pregnant with Amber and we met with our obstetrician I asked if there was a possibility that I might be able to avoid a Caesarean this time. The cells that had forced the operation the first time around had been lazered off and I was informed that there was no medical reason why I couldn't have a natural birth. As soon as I knew this I began to research the statistics. Seventy per cent of women who have a Caesarean with their first child and wish to have a natural birth second time around find they do so successfully. That statistic was good enough for me. I was warned that if I went over nine hours of labour I would have to have an emergency Caesarean as the uterus wall is weakened during a C-section and there is a risk of putting unnecessary stress on the baby. But my sister, my mum and my cousin had all had short uncomplicated labours so I was hoping that it was something that ran in the family.

I really wanted to avoid having another Caesarean. I wanted to feel my baby being born. The thing that spurred me on more than anything was the knowledge that if I had a natural birth I would be able to pick my new baby up and nurse her myself without having to wait for someone else to do it for me. Also, in my experience, with a Caesarean all the pain comes after and the effects last for weeks, but with a natural birth the pain is all during the labour. Afterwards there might be after-pains as your uterus contracts (yes, I winced then too), and if you've had an epidural you may suffer headaches for a few days, but at least you can pick up your baby and carry on in something resembling a normal fashion. With a Caesarean you have to remember that you have had a fairly major operation and need to treat it as such. Rest might be a laughable idea with a newborn baby, but rest is what you need if you've undergone a C-section. I need to stress at this point that this is *my* experience. Some women would much prefer to have a Caesarean over a normal birth and find that the certainty that a C-section offers gives them comfort and allows them to feel in control; I can only talk about how I personally felt.

I also found on my visit to the labour ward at the hospital that the midwives were very pro-natural birth and were supportive of me trying to give birth myself second time around. This spurred me on, these women help deliver hundreds of babies every year, surely, I thought, they know what they're talking about.

Birth 'Advice'

When you are pregnant, well-meaning people want to tell you their stories and if you're like me you'll have soaked up their advice like a sponge. I wanted to know what anyone else who'd gone through pregnancy and motherhood had to say. But you might very well be sick to death of being offered advice, even when you've not asked for it, and for that reason I am reticent about giving out my own pearls of wisdom. However, I suppose as you are reading this book I might be at liberty to at least assume that you won't slam the book shut in indignation and take it back for a refund if I do touch a little on what I wish I'd been told before I'd had both of my birth experiences. Feel free to take it or leave it, but here goes …

♡ Please don't panic. I wound myself up into such a frenzy when I was nearing my due date with Amber and knew that I would be aiming for a natural labour that I put unnecessary stress on myself. In the event, my fears were misplaced. Yes, it was tough and painful and all of the things you'd expect from labour, but it was nowhere near as terrifying as I had wound myself up to believe. The fear of the unknown had led me to imagine all sorts of horrible outcomes that were unfounded and the actual labour itself was a lot easier than I'd imagined.

♡ You don't have to be a hero. Ask for pain relief as and when you need it. Don't think that you have to suffer a 24-hour labour with nothing more than a bit of gas and air and a Tens machine. Also on this note, you cannot guarantee that there will be an anaesthetist to hand to administer an epidural the moment that your labour pains become unbearable. In some hospitals you have to book in advance to have an anaesthetist present. In others they may well be there, but if an emergency Caesarean suddenly needs to take place on the labour suite and you have to wait, you'll have to make do with alternative pain relief such as pethidine or the classic method of biting on your partner's arm and hoping for the best. So don't be afraid to ask about your options. Your midwife should be able to answer your queries before the big day.

♡ You can go back on your plans. If you get to the big day and you've been adamant that you want a certain part of your birth to be looked after in a particular way and then it doesn't feel right, speak up. I say this because I had initially thought that I might quite like to try a water birth with Amber. I know quite a few people who swear by it; Davina McCall for one is a big advocate. After some thought I decided that I quite fancied the idea of serenely swimming around in a pool and my baby being born into the water – a far more comforting entrance into the world for her than popping out and gasping for air, after all she had been in the dark watery comfort of the womb for nine months. A couple of weeks before my due date I went to the hospital to re-familiarise myself with the labour suite. I was taken into the room where the birthing pool was housed and I knew straight away that it just didn't feel right. There were no windows; it was airless and stuffy. The walls were painted navy blue and made the room feel dark and oppressive. And then I saw it: dangling over the pool was a harness attached to a winch. Gone was my idyllic Blue Lagoon fantasy. Instead I had the awful image of myself thrashing around pregnant and naked and being winched up like Free Willy while a room full of medical staff looked on in horror. I decided there and then that water births weren't for me — although I'm sure that the experience would have been very different than what I'd imagined!

Feeling the Baby Kick for the First Time

I think I was about 20 weeks pregnant when I first felt Phoebe kick. I was lying on the settee watching TV (*Birth Stories*, most likely). At first I didn't know what the tickly, butterfly-wings-fluttering-against-the inside-of-my-belly sensation was. Could it be trapped air? Or one Krispy Kreme doughnut too many? Or just something I'd imagined? I paused the TV for a moment and waited to see if something else happened and there it was again, stronger this time. I put my hand to my stomach; that was definitely a kick! I shouted Vernon in from the kitchen to come and feel. He ran in excited, but, typically, as many other mums have attested, couldn't feel anything and so it would be for at least another week. Every time I excitedly exclaimed that the baby had kicked Vernon would put his hand on my stomach …and feel nothing. I felt as if I was making it up, I just wanted him to be able to feel what I could feel: our baby kicking inside of me. When he finally did feel it he was absolutely elated.

When I had seen our baby on the scan I was excited and overwhelmed, but actually being able to feel her kicking inside of me made me feel totally connected to her. Every time I felt a tiny kick against me it was like she was letting me know she was there. And even though I still didn't *know* that we were having a girl, I still had that feeling that we were. As the weeks went by the kicks became a lot less like fluttering butterfly wings and a lot more like karate kicks. I would lie on the bed and watch in wonder as the imprint of an arm or a leg would momentarily protrude from my stomach. If someone had told me that this would happen before I became pregnant I would have thought that it would be a very strange thing to see, almost alien, but when it's your baby it's just amazing!

With Amber I felt her kick earlier, maybe around the 17 or 18-week mark. This is common in second and subsequent pregnancies. Signs that we might have missed in the first pregnancy and passed off as a bit of trapped wind, we identify straight away the second time around as our little one kicking.

The Second Scan – Time to Find Out the Sex?

The second scan is more detailed that the first. Obviously the first scan is very special because it's the first time you get to actually see your baby, but the second scan gives you so much more detail and it becomes even more of a reality that there is a little person inside of you. While the first scan is a dating scan, where they measure the foetus and give you a due date based on measurements, the second scan is like an MOT for the baby. It is amazing to watch as the doctor checks, among other things, all the fingers and toes, for cleft palate, performs a cranial measurement and looks at the four chambers of the heart.

This is also the time when you can find out the sex of your baby, although I've heard that not all hospitals offer this. The first time around with Phoebe we were adamant we didn't want to know, we really wanted it to be a surprise. The second time around we decided to find out. I was a little hesitant, feeling slightly guilty, sure that I was in some way playing God. I was also fearful of personalizing our little one before we'd even met her. But Vernon was so enthusiastic about finding out that I eventually caved in and admitted I was *desperate* to know! I had to agree that it did seem like the right thing to do. And it would be just our secret. I have heard of couples where one wanted to know and the other didn't so the doctor told only one of them. I don't know how they could keep it a secret for the next

20 weeks; that would take an awful lot of will power. I wouldn't
be able to keep that sort of information secret from Vernon for
more than a day without letting it slip.

We took Phoebe with us, but we knew we couldn't tell her as
she would be so excited that everyone she met would know too,
so as we went into the scan room I whispered to the doctor if he
could write the sex on a piece of paper for us and put it in an
envelope so that we could look at it later. We looked at the image
of our baby and I was giddy with excitement knowing that soon
I would know if it was a boy or a girl. I had a gut feeling that I was
having a boy and as I'd been so adamant that Phoebe was going
to be a girl, and had been proved right, I thought that I must be
right on this occasion too. I stared at the screen to see if I could
fathom myself what sex our baby was. Of course I couldn't.

We were handed the envelope with the precious information
as we left the room and it felt like getting exam results, but a
hundred times more nerve-racking. Vernon was nodding at me
over Phoebe's head ,urging me to open it and whisper to him. I
was doing that wide-eyed tight-lipped 'No' look to him, thinking
that the huge matter of unveiling the sex of our baby deserved
a bit more ceremony than furtive whispering. After all, once we
knew that was it, we knew! Vernon had to get straight off to
work afterwards and I had a meeting so was dropping Phoebe
at nursery. I was to be the keeper of the envelope for the next
few hours and I could feel it burning a hole in my handbag!

Vernon rang me at least every half hour. 'Open it!' he coaxed.
I wasn't having any of it. What was I going to do, open it at the
traffic lights and announce it on loudspeaker. I told him to be
patient. That evening Vernon didn't get back until seven and
I was busy getting Phoebe ready for bed, so we didn't open it

then. I put it in a bedside drawer and a little bit of me hoped that Vernon would forget all about it. It felt like going hunting for your presents before Christmas Day. You're really triumphant, but then you know what you're getting, there's no more surprises and there's no going back!

We were in bed when Vernon remembered. He jumped out of bed. 'Get the envelope!' So I went and got it and we opened it, my stomach doing somersaults. We both looked at the piece of paper, squinted and then looked again. The doctor's handwriting was so bad that we couldn't read it! Vernon took it and inspected it further. He smiled. 'It's a girl' he said. A girl? I couldn't believe it I was sure I was having a boy, but I didn't care, I was delighted: two little girls, a little sister for Phoebe, how lovely. Vernon had a brother and I had a sister; there seemed to be a synergy to this, I should have known.

The mistake I did make was telling my mum and sister that we'd found out the sex. They both tried every sneaky trick in the book to find out whether we were having a boy or a girl. Every time we mentioned a girl's name we liked we had to counterbalance it with a boy's name. I was careful to always say 'it', but if the occasional 'he' or 'she' popped out then I would have to assure everyone that I wasn't giving the game away and that I did slip up and say both sexes. I was on pins trying not to put my foot in it. In the end I got used to saying 'it' and Vernon and I didn't even say 'she' to one another. Phew! Pressure or what?

The Third Trimester
Weeks 28 to Due Date

Baby Paraphernalia

Choosing a Pram

Now is the time that you can start buying all your essential pieces of baby kit in earnest. Choosing a pram especially can be a mind-boggling experience. When I was a child prams came in two forms: the sort that Wendy Craig pushed around in *The Nanny*, Victorian numbers with big heavily sprung wheels that were flat-lying for younger babies; and the upright buggy sort that folded up so you could get on the bus with them. Nowadays there is a pram for every lifestyle. Do you want a 'travel system'? That is, an interchangeable flat-lying pram, car-seat and upright buggy? Do you want three wheels or four? Do you travel and need it to fit into an overhead compartment? Do you do a lot of walking and need something with tractor wheels that you could go off-roading with? Are you planning a second child soon or having twins? In which case you'll need a double buggy and if that's the case, do you want them to sit side by side or one in front of the other? A simple trip to Mothercare to look at the dizzying array of prams can leave you breathless!

It is hard to visualize your needs before you know how your life will be when you have your new baby. But buying a pram is something you probably want to get out of the way before the baby comes, so try and work out what you might want to do with your pram, being as realistic as possible, and work from there. One thing to try to avoid is to be drawn in by fashion. Just because everyone else is buying a £600 interchangeable three-wheeler doesn't mean you have to. It might not be what you

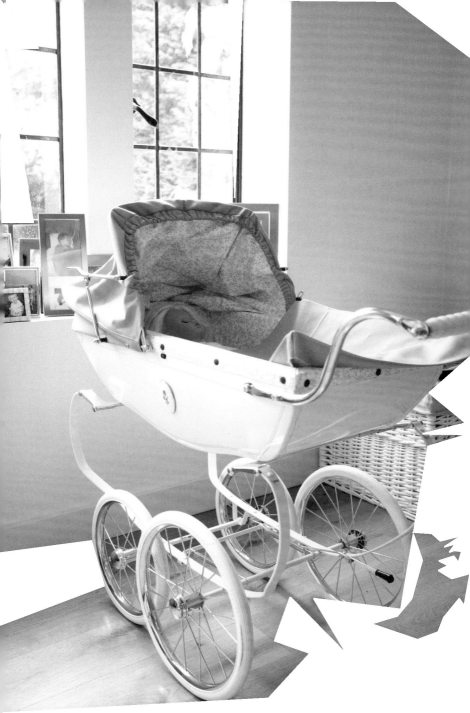

need, and just remember that it will be covered in milk and food in no time anyway. The first pram we got was a Bugaboo; it looked great and did everything we needed it to do except that the wheels were huge and it was hard to carry around and get in and out of the back of the car. This time around we have gone for a Mamas & Papas Pliko Pramette. I read up on the subject and with the advantage of hindsight knew what I needed my new pram to do. It is fairly lightweight, the wheels aren't too big, it has interchangeable bits meaning I can attach the car seat to it and, importantly for Vernon, the handles extend so that he can push the pram without kicking the tyres as he walks along. We also have a carry cot that attaches and doubles up as a Moses basket if we go anywhere to stay.

My main priority with two children is to keep packing to a minimum if we go anywhere, and to be able to fold the pram down and pack it away easily while jugging two children. This may sound obvious, but I think it's worth saying, having stood at the door to my flat nearly in tears and unable to fold down my pram while some attendant paparazzi snapped away as I struggled (they could have taken a picture and then offered to help at least!).

Make sure you can fold your pram away before you take your baby out in it for the first time. One mum I was speaking to about this found herself stranded on a cold January day with her three-day-old baby by a river in the rain, unable to get her baby either out of the straps or the fancy pram folded down and in the car. She couldn't get hold of anyone that might be able to help and in desperation rang an old colleague whose number was in her phone, on the grounds that he was a dad and might have some knowledge of prams. He saved the day, but not before a few tears.

When Phoebe outgrew her Bugaboo we bought a Maclaren buggy. It was light weight, relatively inexpensive, had a good rain cover, reclines so that your baby/toddler can sleep and folds down easily. When ever you see Brad Pitt out and about with the kids he's pushing a Maclaren, so if it's good enough for Brad and Ange it's good enough for me. We'll be using that again when Amber is a bit older.

On the subject of having two children, it is tempting, if they are close in age, to buy a double buggy, but often a buggy board is a cheaper and easier solution if the older child is walking. This is something that clips onto the back of your existing pram and allows your toddler to be close to you, but has the freedom to stand up – it also means that you don't have to lug around a cumbersome double buggy. It isn't so great if you do a lot of walking, as your little one can get tired standing up on the board, but for short journeys and popping to the shops it works quite well.

Travel Cot

Travel cots come in all shapes and sizes and again it is worth thinking about how much time your little one will spend in one before you splurge on something that might only be used twice a year. One thing we did get, that I think is worth mentioning because it was such a genius buy, was a Samsonite pop-up travel cot. It's lightweight, packs away to almost nothing and pops out without the faffing that so often comes with travel cots. Also it only costs around £30. It is only suitable until around six months, after which we used a conventional travel cot, but for those first few months it came in really hand and is definitely one of my star baby buys since having the girls.

Monitors

Monitors are a bit like one-way walkie talkies. You put one in your baby's room and the other stays with you wherever you happen to be in the house. It allows you to hear if your baby is crying or upset, without running up the stairs every two minutes to check that everything is all right. With Phoebe we had a normal monitor. One half of it went in the bedroom, to pick up any noises she made, and the other went downstairs wherever we were so that we could hear her. The only problem was that any noises that Phoebe made we responded to by running to her room and seeing that she was okay. We began to think that we were perpetuating the problem of Phoebe's broken sleep by never allowing her to learn how to settle herself properly.

With this in mind, and Amber on the way, we decided to take a different tack with the baby monitor this time around. We bought a video monitor. It was an all-singing all-dancing contraption that allowed us to see our baby as she slept and would mean that, hopefully, when she cried we would be able to see on the screen whether it was a genuine cry because she was distressed, or a can-someone-come-and-play-with-me-please-cry, which we could ignore and then she could settle herself. But it didn't quite work out that way. The screen is really prone to interference and anytime Amber cries the screen has a tendency to pixelate just when we need to see her so we found we were still doing the dash to the bedroom. Not only that, but the inbuilt night-light would flood the bedroom with light at ever whimper! So we've gone back to the old-school aural monitor. The one we've plumped for this time is an Avent monitor and has a great facility on it where you can talk back to your baby to comfort her without having to go in the room and disturb her. There's a button you press to speak (so that she isn't subjected to *Corrie* and her parents chatting all evening) and so far it's working out really well.

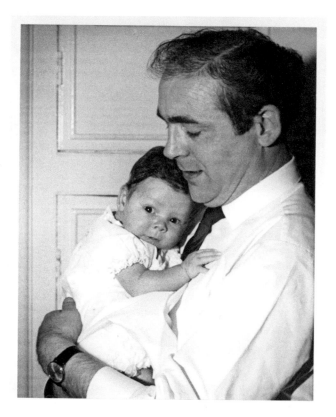

Me and my dad

Buying Clothes for Your Baby

As we didn't know whether we were having a boy or girl, the first time round I only allowed myself one specific baby clothing purchase before Phoebe was born, and that was after David Dickenson's wife had looked at my stomach and predicted I was having a girl. It was a beautiful white lace dress from Monsoon that I hid under the bed so as not to tempt fate. I did of course buy babygros, scratch mitts, and a hat, all in neutral white, for when our little one arrived and we brought her home from the hospital. The only trouble was that I had bought everything in 0–3 months and poor Phoebe left the hospital drowning in her garments. You couldn't even see her in her car seat; she just looked like a pile of clothes. So when I was going into hospital to have Amber I made sure that I had enough newborn-size clothes to at least last a week. I would suggest that when you buy newborn clothes it is best to resist the temptation to buy too many – they may look absolutely adorable, but your baby will grow out of them within a few weeks, so just get the basics. Even now, Amber is only eight weeks old and I've already discarded her newborn-sized clothes. But before I give them away, Phoebe has claimed them to dress her dolls in.

As we knew we were having a girl the second time around I went girl clothes crazy in celebration, almost immediately after the second scan. I had to be careful though, as Vernon and I had decided that we didn't want anyone else to know the sex of our baby, not even our parents. I went to Mamas & Papas and stocked up on tonnes of their gorgeous girly range: darling dresses and little socks with frills around the top. In Marks &Spencer I stocked up on little summer dresses and in Designers at Debenhams I found a cute little tennis dress from Jasper Conran and sparkly sequinned and butterfly-embellished outfits from Matthew Williamson. Zara for Kids also have a great baby range, I particularly loved their A-line dresses; the clothes are quite reasonable yet the styling makes them look designer. The temptation was everywhere to buy clothes by the trolley-load. Even now I try to resist, but it's futile and Amber already has more clothes that I do.

Something I would suggest doing with close family and friends – who hopefully won't mind you being honest – is ask that if they are going to buy clothes as a gift for the next baby that they do so in size 6-12 months, or even older. Otherwise you will end up with a wardrobe full of clothes that it is hard to get through in the first few months and soon you'll have to go out and buy new clothes. This way they still get to buy a gift that they know will be worn, and you will have clothes for your baby for longer.

Style in the
Third Trimester

I always went with the theory that it was better to emphasise the bump than hide it. I felt that in trying to disguise my bump in a Demis Roussos-type tent top only made me look fat and I didn't want to look fat I wanted to look pregnant. The one concession to bump-disguising clothing was the second time around with Amber. I would put a baggy granddad shirt on which worked really well with leggings and pumps or gladiator sandals.

I lived in my American Apparel jean leggings right up until the birth with both pregnancies, but there were some non-pregnancy clothes that couldn't see me past the 28-week mark, no matter how many sizes I went up. As you near your due date your ribcage, as well as your belly, expands and it is difficult to find clothes to fit that aren't specifically tailored for a pregnant figure. I found Isabella Oliver and Mamas & Papas to be great for stretchy dresses that were comfortable, yet stylish, and fitted in all the right places. There were times, of course, when nothing seemed to fit and I wanted to throw all my tops across the room, but I would eventually calm down and find something. I used to try to cheer outfits up with lots of statement jewellery too.

When I was pregnant with Phoebe, empire line dresses were big, which are great for a pregnant belly, but this time around I had to be a little bit more creative. Boyfriend jackets teamed with vests and leggings work well, as do little summer dresses. I think the best advice is to try things on as they hang differently when you're pregnant and your shape changes from week to week.

Sometimes though, if I was attending a big bash where the dress code was full-on glamour, I would come out in an axiety rash. I had more than my fair share of 'I've Nothing to Wear' moments. When I was 32 weeks pregnant with Amber I was presenting an award at the BAFTAs. Nothing I owned seemed to hang correctly and I was beginning to feel a little deflated. Then I remembered a dress that I had ordered from net-a-porter. com as a treat for when the baby was born and I dug it out. It was by a designer called Phillip Lim and was a short, long sleeved dress with ruffles down the middle. I knew that it was either going to look totally wrong or just right. I was pleased to discover that it worked. The ruffles accentuated my bump and disguised the fact that I was pregnant at the same time, and it seemed to cling in the right places – the first thing I'd tried on that had managed that. I was so pleased. I teamed it with some gladiator style heels and I felt confident enough to skip out of the door and on to national TV. Rob Brydon even asked me if I was really pregnant, but I think he was just being kind.

Bye Bye Feet

Around the eight month of pregnancy it is time to say goodbye
to your feet. You might be able to see them when you're sitting
down, but forget it when you're standing up. Your feet also
become impossible to get to, which for me (someone who likes
to keep on top of chipped toenail varnish) became a nightmare.
I would wrestle around trying to get the nail varnish brush near
my toes; attempting to reach and paint each toe in one quick
fell swoop before I was propelled backwards by my bump like
someone having a fight on a space hopper. This resulted in each
coat being more unsatisfactory than the last and ultimately
me walking around with nail varnish so badly applied that
it looked as though I'd painted one foot with the other.

To Wax or
Not to Wax?

As we near our due date most general female upkeep becomes almost impossible. Trying to shave my legs was a similar debacle to painting my toes, and Vernon offered to help. Now there are some things, as far as I'm concerned, that Vernon shouldn't need to do in his capacity as husband, and shaving any part of me is one of them thank you very much. In fact, he shouldn't even need to *know* that I shave my legs. Let's leave men to think that we women are hairless creatures with no need for deodorant, and not much call for a toilet either, and let us get on with our own grooming in private I say. Having said all this, trying to do anything with my bikini line on my own became a laughable exercise. With my first pregnancy, because I was having an elective Caesarean I knew that shaving was not an option, but a necessity. My obstetrician offered to do it, which quite frankly is above and beyond the call of duty, and I was far too heavily pregnant to be nipping out for a Brazilian, so I tackled it myself with the aid of some depilatory cream, a razor and a mirror. Let's just say the results didn't make me want to change careers and become a beauty therapist!

One thing I would say, as there are often rumours flying around to the contrary, is that if you are planning a normal birth there is no need to worry about shaving or waxing anything unless you so wish. It used to be the norm for birthing ladies to be expected to be cleanly shorn, like a plucked chicken, but those days are gone, so you can save yourself a lot of time, worry and pain in that department!

Grocery Shopping

If you are like me and are responsible for the weekly shop
(I think most women are or we'd end up with cupboards full
of Pop Tarts and Pot Noodles) squeezing shopping in to our
routine can be a bind as we near our due date. Actually, I need
to admit something here. I LOVE grocery shopping, but I know
I'm in a minority – I prefer to pick and choose my own nectarines
without someone having manhandled them for me! Walking
around the aisles, planning what I'm going to cook for the
week and what I can feasibly fit in our freezer, which is always
bursting at the seams, is a joy to me. It's not just when I'm
pregnant that I go into this 'must stockpile food mentality'.
I just love having a well-stocked kitchen. Anyone who's been
to our house and opened our fridge will tell you that there's
always a risk of a food avalanche.

So, as you can imagine, I'm no stranger to our local Waitrose.
But even I acknowledge that grocery shopping isn't the easiest
thing to undertake when you are heavily pregnant or have a
newborn baby. Even getting out of the house with your teeth
brushed and your coat on the right way round is a challenge.
So if, unlike me, you see grocery shopping as a chore, try to make
life easier for yourself in the months before you give birth and
organize an online shopping service.

I believe it's quite simple once you get the hang of it
(although you need to watch out for baby brain and avoid
ordering six kilos of bananas instead of six bananas), and it
really does make life easier. The beauty of online shopping
is (obviously) that you don't have to leave the house. Most

supermarkets offer this service now and it means you don't have to lug hundreds of nappies and tins of formula as well as your weekly shopping and a newborn baby around in the cold. It also means that you can have just have basics delivered to your house every week, leaving you to top up with stuff that you need throughout the week without feeling like a packhorse. There is usually a charge of about £5 for delivery, depending on the supermarket, but it seems worth it to save yourself the hassle of venturing out. That's if, unlike me, you see it as hassle. Even as I'm writing this, I'm thinking of all the lovely things I can put in my trolley if I pop to Waitrose later. I just need to feed Amber first, take the dogs for a walk, finish this chapter and get there before picking Phoebe up from school ...

Decorating
the Nursery

With Phoebe we held back on decorating the nursery until
I was well into my third trimester. I think it is natural to be
a bit superstitious about these things and not to tempt fate
by going ahead and doing the house up to include your new
baby until he or she is safely in your arms. We finally decided
to paint the nursery white and bought all the furniture basics:
wardrobe, drawers, cot and a broderie anglaise Moses basket
that I thought might be a bit frilly if we did have a boy, even
with the evidence to the contrary, but I quite liked and it went
with the room.

There are so many places to buy baby furniture now that it
can become a bit bamboozling. You begin to wonder if you need
a cot bed or just a cot. Do you need an adult-sized wardrobe or
a kid-sized wardrobe? Once the baby is here, and soon becomes
a boisterous toddler, you will realize that whether you have
bought the furniture from Harrods or Ikea it will soon get drawn
on and charged at and that it is best to just be as practical as
possible. Having said that, on the flipside of practical I did treat
our baby (me really, it just looked so gorgeous in the shop) to
a rocking horse. The other big treat I allowed myself was some
Flower Fairies furniture from a shop called Dragons of Walton
Street in Chelsea. They are beautiful heirloom pieces and
something the girls can keep for ever. Dragons sells hand-
crafted and painted toys – it's where Princess Diana used to
buy toys for her sons – and anytime I'm in Chelsea I pop in

to have a look and lose myself in this truly magical toyshop. If you do nip by say hello to Adam and Sally for me, they are as priceless as their shop!

There are a few things that I bought and thought would come in really handy, but that I never used; one being a baby bouncer that you hang from the door. It just never seemed to fit or hang correctly and I just had visions of poor Phoebe gathering a bit of speed as she bounced and then launching herself across the living room. I soon consigned the bouncer to a pile of stuff I was taking to the charity shop. Another thing that was used for a few months and then pretty much ignored was the tabletop changer. Once your baby gets to a certain size and begins to show signs of wanting to roll over you don't really want them anywhere other than on the floor when you're changing them. So the tabletop changer gradually became more of a book shelf and I bought a normal changing matt and some towelling change matt toppers from the White Company and found they worked just as well without the worry.

Preparing for the Hospital

Timing the Journey

Around this time we started to think about getting to the hospital in the throes of labour. We didn't do a dummy run as such, but we knew how far it was and what the worst-case scenario would be with regards to traffic. With Phoebe we still lived in London and the hospital was only 20 minutes away, even in heavy traffic. Also, because I knew I was having a Caesarean with Phoebe, we didn't worry too much about the length of time it would take to get to the hospital as it was an operation and I was allotted a time to arrive and for the procedure to begin. With Amber it was different. I was hoping for a natural birth and now we lived outside of London the traffic into the hospital could be unpredictable – anywhere from 40 minutes to an hour and a half in heavy traffic.

Vernon became very anxious about this uncertainty. He was convinced that he was going to have to deliver the baby himself in a motorway lay-by, and that we would end up on *Real Rescues*. Strangely, the more anxious he got about it, the calmer I became. I really hoped I wasn't going to have a prolonged labour as both my mum and sister had had short labours, but I certainly didn't think that our baby would pop out on the hard shoulder. I tried to explain to Vernon that there would be a lot of contractions to go through before the baby made any appearance. Mind you, when I wasn't attempting to appear calm and reassuring I was actually pretty damn petrified myself by the unpredictability of it all.

Vernon and his Role at the Hospital

This might sound a little flippant, but the only real plan I had for Vernon during both births was that he drive me to the hospital and be there to squeeze my hand. I know there are lots of books advising that your partner help massage you and know all of the different positions that you can get in to make the birth easier, but I just wanted him to get me there and to *be* there. Actually, I tell a lie, he was responsible for making sure that the video and the camera were charged and for liaising with our nearest and dearest to let them know as events unfolded.

There is a lot of advice out there about how your partner can help you during your labour and one thing that made us laugh till we cried was the idea of the perineum massage. This is something that is performed, either by yourself or 'your partner' in order to stretch the skin that can often tear during childbirth. Now you may be very forward thinking and not mind your partner massaging the bit between your, and I quote, 'vagina and anus' in the weeks leading up to your birth, but I couldn't think of anything worse! Standing there with one foot up on the chair while Vernon prodded around in a most unromantic fashion? Oh please!

Another thing I read recommended trying not to gain any weight in the final weeks of pregnancy. I am loathed to even write about this on the off chance that someone thinks this is anything like a good idea, but I found it so ridiculous that I wanted to quickly comment on it. One book makes claims that sugar can harden the uterus and make labour more painful (which my doctor later told me was ridiculous) and recommends not eating anything sugary – even *grapes*, for goodness' sake.

If you do have a craving you can allow yourself *one teaspoonful of honey a week*. Hold me back, a whole teaspoon! At the time of reading this I was craving biscuits and chocolate so much that Vernon commented that our cupboards looked like a sweet shop. I wanted pudding and custard and apple pie and cream every hour on the hour. A drop of honey once a week just wasn't going to do it for me.

I mention this because I think that we can easily begin to doubt and punish ourselves, especially if we think that we are in any way being detrimental to our baby. But we also need to be mindful that a lot of advice is subjective; warning you off sweets is one thing, but telling you to watch your weight during pregnancy is another. Apparently two to three stone is the average weight gain and regarded as fairly normal. So I decided to take that particular advice with a pinch of salt (or was that a packet of Hob Nobs?)

Baby Bag

I kept reading about packing a baby bag. The packing of the baby bag seems to take on a mythical status for a lot of mums to be. What to include? Should I pack ten full baby outfits for all weathers, just in case we are kept in for over a week and there happens to be a lot of fire alarms that week? Should I pack a full range of products for myself, including something that will make my skin glisten like the morning dew as I sit there cradling my little one? What about breast pads? Should I pack them? What *are* breast pads anyway? And what are maternity pads exactly? They look like sanitary towels from the seventies, why might I need them?

21/10/2004

The whole thing can become a bit of a nightmare. A mum I know told me she brought her entire make-up bag to the hospital and was applying her full face after 48 hours of no sleep. She thought it might make her look more like herself in the photographs of her and her new baby. She says instead she looked like Bette Davis in *Whatever Happened to Baby Jane?* My advice would be to keep it as simple as possible. Firstly get yourself a loose vest or T-shirt that covers your bum for the actual birth itself. I say this because you will be spending a good few hours knickerless, possibly on all fours, and having just a crop top on might make you feel slightly self-conscious! You will probably discard whatever you wear at the birth afterwards, as even with the best births things can get a little messy, so it's best not to spend a fortune on it, just make sure you are comfortable. Do buy yourself a decent pair of pyjamas or nightie for afterwards though. Once you have your lovely baby in your arms you will probably, after a while, want to get cleaned up and feel as fresh as you possibly can after all that exertion. So something nice and new to put on afterwards is a treat that you can give yourself. Do be mindful that your belly will probably look pretty much as it has for the past few months just after you've given birth, so give yourself some leeway and don't buy lingerie that you hope to fit into one day but choose something that you can fit into now that will make you feel comfortable.

The hardest thing I found to buy was a decent pair of slippers. Every shop I went into seemed to assume that the average slipper buying age was 85. Maybe it is. But as I wasn't heading off to a twilight home just yet I wanted a pair that were comfortable, but didn't make me look like Nora Batty. I finally found some in Marks & Spencer. They were really simple waffled, peep-toe white slippers like the type you get in a health spa. Places that stock nice slippers do seem to be few and far between, but I did notice that The White Company do a great white sheepskin pair that look so comfortable you could curl up and sleep in them. I'd also suggest packing a warm throw or cardigan. Cashmere works really well as it regulates your body temperature. Be sure, if you are breastfeeding, that it opens at the front for easy access.

The next thing on the list is knickers. There seems to be some mystery surrounding birth and knickers. When I was looking for advice on what to pack in my baby bag they seemed to take on some significance that they've never had before in most of the books I read. I couldn't seem to find an explanation anywhere of why knickers that could be worn and then discarded seemed so important at this time. Some books even mentioned disposable knickers – to my horror you can buy them in places like Boots. I personally think you've been through enough during labour to then have to suffer the indignity of slipping on some paper undies afterwards, so pack yourself some 100 per cent cotton undies that you don't mind getting rid of afterwards.

So, this is the reason it is recommended you go to the hospital armed with knickers, disposable or otherwise: after the birth you will have a discharge called 'lochia', which is like a heavy period and stops within six weeks or so. It's no big surprise for anyone who's ever had a period; it just isn't very pleasant and can last a few weeks, although the bleeding does get lighter after a few days. It is advised that you wear only natural fibres because synthetic fibres can cause thrush and as you will no doubt be a little tender down there anyway you won't want anything adding to that tenderness, so cotton is the best option. There we go, knicker mystery over.

You will also want to pack things for your baby but try (as hard as this might be) to keep this to a minimum. Keep in mind that even if, once you have you baby you have to stay in for a few nights, you can always ask someone to bring things to the hospital for you. Here's what I think is useful to pack in a baby bag:

For You:

♡ Your hospital notes and birth plan.

♡ Breast pads. Whether you are breastfeeding or bottle feeding your milk will begin to flow and breast pads help prevent your nipples getting sore by absorbing any excess milk. They also ensure that you don't lactate on your PJs. Grim, but true.

♡ Maternity pads. If you have your baby through natural childbirth then for a few weeks afterwards you will have a period-like discharge. Maternity pads are best as they are bigger so can cope with a very heavy flow and, unlike tampons, they'll help you and your midwife monitor the amount of bleeding (not that you'll be wanting to pop anything up there for a while). So maternity pads are the gentlest solution to this problem.

♡ Cotton knickers (a bumper variety pack to be on the safe side).

♡ Travel-size shampoo, conditioner and shower gel. Deodorant, toothbrush and toothpaste. Hair brush and hair bobble if you have long hair – it's best to have something to keep it out of your face when in labour, it will only get on your nerves.

♡ Face wipes (you won't really feel much like performing a cleanse, tone and moisturize routine) and moisturizer.

♡ Minimal make-up. Mascara, lip balm and perhaps a cream blusher if you're expecting visitors.

♡ A couple of long vests or tops/nighties that cover your bum for the actual labour. Sitting around in just a top with no knickers on, even in labour, is like a terrifying bad dream – talk about feeling vulnerable.

♡ Pyjamas for when you are back on the ward, and a night gown.

♡ A decent pair of slippers, or failing that flip flop-type sandals. A few pairs of socks.

♡ Magazines or a book. Keep your reading light, you won't want or have time to settle down with War and Peace either during or after labour.

♡ A portable DVD player or laptop. Obviously not a necessity, but a few episodes of your favourite box set can help pass a few hours if you are waiting around, but you might want to think carefully about this as things can be stolen from hospitals when you are in the throes of labour. Sad, but true.

♡ Anti-bacterial gel or handwash.

♡ Earplugs so you can cut out the noise of all those lovely newborns exercising their lungs around you as you try to get some well-earned rest.

For Your Baby:

♡ Newborn-size nappies.

♡ 2 packs of scent-free baby wipes or cotton wool to use with water.

♡ 3 x baby grows – newborn size.

♡ 1 x baby hat – newborn size.

♡ 2 x baby socks – newborn size.

♡ 3 x vests – newborn size.

♡ 2 x bibs – newborn size.

♡ A warm blanket or a warm all-in-one if it is cold when you leave hospital. It will be your little one's first time in the outside air, so wrap him or her up well in the winter months.

♡ Bottles and the correct formula if you are bottle feeding.

♡ A car seat - but you only need this when you've been discharged and are ready to take your baby home.

Birth Plan

I decided with both births not to write a birth plan. The first time around I knew that I was having a Caesarean and I had met with the midwives and obstetrician so I didn't feel that there was anything more I could add that would help. The second time around I felt that I had done enough preparation myself beforehand (watching *Birth Stories*, talking to other mums, reading every book and generally panicking) that I felt as prepared as I could be. I suppose my view was that once I was in there, there was little that could be planned for.

With hindsight I can see why a birth plan is a good idea. You can write as little or as much as you want. If the only thing you are absolutely sure of is that you want an epidural then you can write this down, put the paper in with your notes and hand it over to the midwife when you get there. On the other hand, if you have a list of requests, ranging from attempting a water birth to listening to a certain type of music, then put it all down and again hand it to your midwife.

A birth plan is a way of communicating anything specific you would like to happen during the course of your labour, that may otherwise go out of your head once you are in the throes of back-to-back contractions. It also gives you time before the birth to think about how – in an ideal world – you would like your birth to be. You can discuss your thoughts with your midwife beforehand and she might be able to give you some advice on how best to articulate your requests. It can also help your birthing partner as they have something to refer to. As much as you discuss things prior to going into hospital, actually being there and going through the birth can lead to the most organized of couples forgetting everything they had agreed on.

Having said that, it's important to try and keep your mind open to your birth plan changing if you and your baby's needs alter during labour. A birth is something that, ultimately, will take its own course and the idea of a birth 'plan' can seem a misnomer. However, having your own thoughts and ideas about how you would like things to take place is no bad thing and gives you a voice when you might otherwise feel powerless to say anything.

Aches and Pains

Heartburn

I was about seven months pregnant with Phoebe when I first experienced heartburn, and it was excruciating. It felt like I had acid burning in my chest and that made eating difficult. I went back to eating little and often, as I had done when I was suffering from morning sickness, and tried to work out what I could and couldn't take to alleviate the pain. When you are pregnant, over the counter medication becomes such a minefield, as some commonly used medicines such as ibuprofen (Nurofen) aren't safe during pregnancy. I became convinced that I couldn't take anything other than a paracetemol, no matter what was wrong with me. The best thing to do is ask your pharmacist or doctor if you are worried, or call NHS direct on 0845 4647 if you can't get an appointment with your doctor. NHS Direct is a brilliant service and one that becomes invaluable during pregnancy and when you have a new baby. You can speak to someone who can put your mind at rest. Don't forget that your health visitor is also on hand for all manner of questions at this time.

Anyway, back to my heartburn ... it hurt. So I finally discovered that I could have Gaviscon and it did ease the pain for a little while. Everyone kept telling me that heartburn meant I would have a very hairy baby, which of course at the time I took to be an old wives' tale. Though when Phoebe was born she had a thick head of hair! So when I suffered from heartburn again with Amber (it didn't hurt as much this time around though) I wasn't surprised when she was born with hair so thick that she needed her fringe cut. People I passed in the street would stop me and gasp, 'What a hairy baby.' And they weren't wrong!

Sleeping

I always sleep on my side so I was lucky that I could carry on sleeping in the position I was used to when I was pregnant, especially as you are advised not to life flat on your back during the later stages of pregnancy and lying on your front is physically impossible! As I got bigger I found it more comfortable to sleep with a pillow tucked between my legs, it seemed to take some of the pressure off my bump. So my sleeping position never got in the way of a good night's sleep. My bladder on the other hand ...

When we are pregnant our bladders seem to shrink to the size of a pea. At first I would have to get up once in the night, which was annoying enough, but towards the end with both pregnancies it was two and sometimes three times a night. The broken sleep left me exhausted. I always liked to think that it was our body's way of preparing us for having to get up with our babies, but it's actually the fact that by this stage your baby is taking up so much room your bladder can't expand as much as it did. Either way, it would be far nicer if our bodies gave us a break and let us have a night's sleep once in a while before the big day. With my second pregnancy Amber was lying really low from about week 30 onwards and seemed to be pressing on my bladder. So for the last quarter of my pregnancy I felt like I needed the toilet non-stop! Of course if you really do feel like you are going to the toilet *all the time* or if you have a slight stinging sensation, it's worth checking with your doctor that you don't have a urine infection.

Work in the Third Trimester

In the third trimester, with both girls, I was still quite busy work wise. In fact I was still attending meetings, taking calls and checking my emails right up until both of my due dates, but I did try to relax a little. With Amber I started work on this book when I was 37 weeks pregnant. I had also been working on a new beauty range for Marks & Spencer, Daly Beauty, which I was involved in every step of the way from choosing formulations and packaging to making sure the products did what they claimed to do. This all came about when I couldn't find a body cream that I used to buy. I hunted around for something to replace it, but anything with a slight shimmer in it seemed either too oily or too shimmery and I would find my clothes covered in marks – not ideal for live TV. So I decided to see if I could come up with my own range of affordable, yet luxurious body care. My Daly Beauty range was born and I was thrilled to bits when Marks & Spencer agreed to stock the entire range.

I also did voiceover work and promotional photo shoots for the upcoming series of *Strictly*. I was really lucky with the way that I work in that I could have time to myself to organize things for the birth. Hypothetically that is, I still seemed to spend my time sorting things for work and being in contact with people. When you are faced with the prospect of being a new mum and you have worked all your adult life it can be hard to relinquish the responsibility of work and admit that things will be okay if you go off the radar for a bit.

Birth Anxiety

When I was pregnant with Phoebe I wasn't particularly anxious about having a Caesarean. Of course, I was nervous about the prospect of being a mum and having to do things that I'd never done before, but the actual operation I would have to go through didn't give me too much cause for concern. I think this was down to the fact that I knew what date and time I would be going into hospital and there was an element of certainty in the whole procedure. When I was pregnant with Amber, however, and hoping for a natural birth, I began to worry about what lay ahead of me. I was fine for the first half of the pregnancy, but after the second scan, with a burgeoning bump, things began to feel very real and the thought that childbirth was looming began to terrify me. I can only think now that it was the fear of the unknown. All I had to go on were the stories that other mums told me, and because I was so insistent that I wanted warts-and-all truth from people then that was what I got. I heard every horror story going and I hoovered them up, longing for the next story so that I could be armed with as many different worse case scenarios as possible. I think this is why I became such an avid fan of *Birth Stories*, it was my on-tap source of what I would potentially experience. But in arming myself with the knowledge of so many different possibilities I scared myself witless. I worried constantly; the only time I felt calm and Zen-like was when Vernon expressed his extreme nervousness. One moment I would be telling myself that everything would be fine, she'd slip out and I'd barely notice; the next I would be panicking that I might give birth on all fours, crawling to the hospital doors, as had happened to my sister – actually, she did manage to make it inside, but she had been on all fours in the car park nonetheless. Knowing my luck someone would have a camera phone to hand; I could just see the flattering picture in the gossip magazines. Then I would worry about the birth itself, what if it was horrendous? What if I ripped from ear to ear? What if I went through hours of labour only to have to go through a Caesarean anyway? That would be the worst scenario of all as far as I was concerned.

You may be reading this and squirming and thinking, thanks, that's cheered me up a bundle and really stopped my poor frayed mother-to-be nerves jangling. Well, here's the thing: the birth was nowhere near as bad as I had imagined it would be. In fact, had I known how comparatively easy it was going to be – compared to my first experience of childbirth – I certainly wouldn't have worked myself up into a such tizz about it.

The Final Week

As your due date approaches you know you are on the last leg of
your pregnancy journey. You have childbirth to go through and at
the end of it there will be a new life that you are bringing into the
world. The prospect of all this can be quite overwhelming. For me
the final week of both my pregnancies was quite daunting. I did
at least know, with both births, the date I was to go into hospital.
With Phoebe it was because I was having a Caesarean; with
Amber, because I had previously had a Caesarean, it was explained
to me that I would be given a date to be induced if I didn't go
into labour naturally. The fact that I had an actual date to go into
hospital to have both girls was a comfort in one respect, but on
the other hand it made it even more nerve-racking knowing that
my baby would be here within a week. It also felt like a bit of a
limbo period. I wasn't working as such with Amber, but I was still
checking emails, finalizing my beauty product line, thinking about
future work commitments and writing notes for this book. No
one reasonably expects you to be particularly productive the
week before you are due to give birth – if they do they are some
sort of sadistic slave driver – but I felt I needed to keep busy for
my own sanity. The house was scrubbed, all the support I thought
that we'd need was in place, and there wasn't much else I could do
only wait for the day to come around that I would have my baby.

With Phoebe I kept looking around our flat and thinking I can't
believe there's going to be a baby here. Then Vernon and I would
have simultaneous panics, becoming, as I recall, preoccupied with
the thought of bathing the baby when it arrived. How do you
actually bathe a baby? How do you hold the head so it doesn't

flop about? They like water, don't they? They've been swimming about in it for months – so can they go underwater? It seemed like a potential minefield that could only be negotiated through a process of trial and error.

With Amber I tired to remember how I'd been as I approached Phoebe's birth and to calm myself, but I couldn't really relax and enjoy the week I had before she arrived as I just wanted the day to be here and to get on with it. I was on pins – we both were – I just wanted to meet that little baby I'd fallen in love with since seeing her heartbeat on that very first scan.

Preparing for the Birth

I had my bag packed and we knew the most direct route to the hospital. With Amber I had decided that I wasn't going to use a Tens machine and that I'd rather not try and administer pain relief myself, but leave it to the professionals. With Phoebe I was mentally preparing for the operation and with Amber I was trying to allay my constantly rising panic and remember my breathing techniques. But there was something else I did, and having talked to a few other mums about this and finding they did something similar I feel that I can own up it, I had my roots done and, wait for it ... a pedicure! It might sound like madness, but I thought while I might come out of it looking like I'd been dragged though a hedge backwards, I certainly wasn't going in there looking that way. I think it was about feeling in control, at least a little, as I went into a situation that I invariably would have little control over. The only thing that prevented me going the hole hog and having a full manicure was that I'd been told that with an elective Caesarean (as I had with Phoebe) the midwife places a clip on your fingernail to monitor the blood; something that could be slightly hampered by three coats of Rouge Noir. It seems a bit daft, writing about it now, but when all dignity goes out of the window it somehow felt like I was hanging on to a teeny bit of my identity.

The
Births

Both births were so entirely different that I am going to write about them separately, as I feel that trying to describe them as one event would be confusing to read. So here it is, the bit that if I was reading this book I would have turned to in the book shop for all the gory details: the birth stories.

Phoebe: The Caesarean

We checked into the hospital on Saturday morning, at 7.30 a.m. for my elective Caesarean. Vernon was nervous and excited and I was just plain nervous. I couldn't believe we were actually going to meet our baby that very day. There weren't many people around at that time and it was quite a calm experience to begin with.

I was fitted with something that would monitor the baby's heartbeat – a sensor strapped to your bump and plugged into a machine – and then the anaesthetist came in to administer the epidural. This proved rather traumatic. I have quite a bony back and could feel every inch of the needle as it entered my spine. Also, to make matters worse, he had to make two attempts at actually getting the needle in; all the while I was thinking, one wrong move and I'll be paralyzed. Anaesthetists are highly trained specialists who perform this injection hundreds of times a year, but it doesn't stop you worrying about the one in a million chance of it going wrong and what the consequences of that would be. Vernon and I caught one another's eye, we were both worried, but trying to be brave for one other.

We were taken through to theatre and Vernon was gowned up. The epidural began to work. It was an odd feeling, like a spreading warmth that numbed as it travelled from the tops of my legs up to my chest bone. I looked around the operating theatre; it all seemed so clinical, which of course it was. I think the oddest thing about having a Caesarean was the speed with which it all happened. Once I was in the theatre the obstetrician made an incision across the bottom of my bump, and within minutes he was rummaging around inside me. Even though the whole area was anaesthetized I could still sense what was going on: a bit like when you go to the dentist to have a tooth taken out, but far more surreal. You can't feel the pain, but you know that the dentist is pulling at you in order to free the tooth. The best way I can describe the sensation as the doctor felt around to pull our baby into the world was like having a builder with huge boots on, inside me, pulling at random bits from the wall of my womb as he stomped about.

Vernon, who was watching all this, described what he was seeing as looking like 'finest steak'. I don't know how he didn't faint, or at least go off steak for life! Then suddenly the obstetrician seemed happy that whatever he was doing was working and he hoisted Phoebe into the world. My beautiful baby daughter was suddenly here. At this stage, of course, we didn't even know we had a daughter. Vernon looked at the doctor and asked, 'What is it?' To which he rather inappropriately replied, 'It's a pink one'. We both looked at one another: did he really just say that? The biggest moment of our lives and the doctor is cracking funnies. He quickly corrected himself and said, 'It's a girl'. We were both delighted, but in hindsight he could have handled such an important moment with more sensitivity.

We were both ecstatic, but a moment later, as the cord was cut and Phoebe was weighed, I began to look around the room nervously wondering if something was wrong. She hadn't cried, newborns were meant to cry, weren't they? You see it on films, they slap the baby to make them cry, not that I wanted anyone to raise a hand to my precious daughter. We were quickly reassured that everything seemed to be fine. They then placed Phoebe in my arm and I held her. My own baby that I'd been carrying around and talking to and wanting so much to be here finally was. I was so happy, but I wasn't allowed to hold her for long. One of the midwives explained that babies born by Caesarean do not naturally expel all of the mucus in the way that babies born through the birth canal do. So they would have to take her away from me to clear her passages and put her under observation. I didn't know anything about this and it panicked me to think that I would be separated from her so soon after giving birth. Was she okay? Where was she? When would I see her? I didn't know what to expect and this not knowing frightened me

Vernon went with Phoebe and I was left on a trolley in a room for 45 minutes on my own under a foil sheet like the ones you see the runners wrapped in after the London Marathon. I could hear other children crying from other rooms and wondered where my little one was. I had no husband, no baby and I felt that I wasn't being told what was going on. As I lay there my body went into shock. I was shaking and my legs were involuntarily banging against the sides of the hospital trolley, probably due to the after-effects of the epidural or simply the birth itself, I was terrified.

I was finally wheeled upstairs to a room where Vernon joined me and put my mind, at least a little, at rest about Phoebe. It wouldn't be long until she was here and I could hold her, he assured me. In the corner of the room there was a phone that began ringing. At this point we hadn't spoken to any of our parents, so when Vernon picked up the phone and a voice said, 'Hello, this is Tess's mum. I'm just ringing to say congratulations'. Vernon couldn't believe what he was hearing, especially the accent he was hearing. It was some journalist with a Home Counties accent who hadn't even considered that my mum might have a northern accent – if she was going to have the bare-faced cheek to impersonate her she might as well get the region right! Vernon slammed the phone down. We were in shock, how did someone pretending to be my mum get through to our room before we'd even managed to tell my mum? As you can imagine we weren't best pleased about this intrusion. After all I was still feeling extremely vulnerable, as a C-section is a major operation.

We calmed down about this and rang our real mums to tell them the news. My mum was in Marks & Spencer buying a chicken (amazing what you remember) and kept her voice down because she obviously thought that even the news that you are a grandparent for the first time couldn't be shouted about in the fresh meat section of Marks & Spencer. Vernon's mum was ecstatic and announced, 'Right, we're getting Syl (my mum) and we're coming down.' They were at the hospital in less than three and a half hours, laden down with 'It's a Girl!' balloons and pink banners. Three and a half hours door-to-door is some sort of record, but nothing was stopping them from seeing their first grandchild.

Phoebe had been brought to my room over an hour after I had her. I was so happy to finally have my baby in my arms and to be able to cradle and hold her to my skin; having her here just felt like the most natural thing in the world. When our parents arrived it was lovely to see them with Phoebe, they were so proud and just wanted to hold her. Those few hours with us all there, with Phoebe so tiny and new, are such precious memories for me.

That night, and the following nights, Vernon stayed on a mattress on the floor. He only went home for one night during my stay in hospital. The mattress, Vernon said, was almost entirely made up of springs and was about five foot seven in length, which didn't quite accommodate his six foot four frame. I think he had the most uncomfortable few night's sleep of his life, but he didn't care because he was sleeping next to his beautiful daughter. I wasn't exactly wallowing in comfort myself. I still had an epidural in my back and a catheter (lovely) so I was constantly attached to something. On the second day my best friend Orla came to visit. She ran in excitedly and hugged me tightly, knocking my epidural out. To this day she swears she didn't, but very quickly I began to feel the pain where my stitches were. When the nurse came to remove my drain later that day she berated me for being a drama queen as I winced and squealed my way through the procedure and became hot and feverish from the pain. Once she had finished she realized that I was actually telling the truth and that the epidural wasn't in correctly and I could feel everything. I have never felt pain like that in my life, and I can say that now having gone through natural childbirth!

As the days in hospital wore on I began to become quite upset by the fact that I couldn't just pick Phoebe up and hold her, and that someone had to pass her to me. Having

30/5/2009

a Caesarean meant that I was now quite limited in what I could do. I knew that I needed to try and move or walk as much as I could, but it still hurt and I didn't have the freedom to pick up my baby. I felt that I shouldn't have to rely on other people, but I had to. I knew that next time, if I had the option, I would definitely try and have a natural childbirth. I know so many women who have had very positive experiences of giving birth by Caesarean, but it seems to me that with this method all the pain comes after.

When we returned home the problems continued. I couldn't bend over the bath properly without wincing with pain, and getting the buggy up and down three flights of stairs or carrying the car seat to the car was also very painful. I wasn't allowed to drive for six weeks either. The lack of independence in those early days really got me down. But on the flipside I was ecstatic to be a mum, I did have a healthy baby and I knew that I was healing well so I tried as much as I could to look to the positive.

Amber:
The Natural Birth

I was told by the obstetrician that I would be induced earlier than my due date, which meant that unless Amber came early I wouldn't go into labour naturally. As I have mentioned before, this gave me a little bit of reassurance and a feeling that at least I knew by that date my baby would be with me. She didn't want to go over that time, my doctor said, as it could have put pressure on my Caesarean scar. We were given a few date options, a little less than a week before my actual due date, and we chose Saturday 30 May. There was a bit of me that wasn't happy with the idea of playing God and deciding which date my little girl would arrive, but then I quickly realized it was all for her safety. Also, knowing the date, I would be induced gave a little bit of certainty to proceedings – I was still gripped with the fear of the unknown!

The day before I was to go into hospital to be induced the obstetrician had recommended that I have a 'cervical sweep'. The name itself was enough to scare me rigid. Someone, brush in hand, sweeping around my cervix? No thank you. I was later to find out that it had nothing to do with the Dick van Dyke in *Mary Poppins* image I had in my mind, and in fact meant that the obstetrician would 'sweep' her fingers around the cervix to dislodge the membranes surrounding my baby from the cervix (I'm not sure what was worse, my imaginings or reality!). If it all goes to plan then this releases hormones called prostaglandins, which can kick start labour.

This procedure has a better chance of working if the cervix is softened and ripe at the time it is performed. So from week 32 onwards I had a cervical examination every two weeks to see if my cervix was softening up, but I know that not all women have such regular check ups in this department. I found this examination uncomfortable and at times downright painful. One week, as I was squirming through the procedure, the obstetrician said to me that the pain was nothing compared to a cervical sweep. I think these were intended as words of comfort, but it had the reverse effect. I just began to live in fear of the dreaded sweep: I wasn't looking forward to this one little bit. I looked up 'cervical sweep' on the Internet and there was mixed stories; some women felt a lot of pain, bled afterwards and had to take painkillers, other women barely felt a thing.

The morning of the sweep I called the obstetrician. It was 90°F (32°C) outside and it was a Friday, so the idea of driving to London in busy traffic in the blistering heat to be prodded and poked wasn't something I relished – especially as I was booked in to be induced anyway the following day. On the other hand, if she said it was something that was worthwhile and could bring on natural labour then I was all for it. So when my obstetrician said 'I think it might help' I wasn't about to argue – Vernon and I got in the car and made our way to the doctor's. As we were driving along we both realized that I hadn't brought my hospital bag or made any real arrangements should I go into spontaneous labour. Oh dear. I had visions of Vernon running up and down Oxford Street in abject panic trying to piece together the necessary bits for a labouring mum – I could just see it now, I'd end up with shoulder pads instead of breast pads.

When we arrived we couldn't find a car park space anywhere. So I told Vernon to stay in the car and that I would attend the sweep alone. Actually I was glad to be going in on my own as I thought I was going to be howling in pain. From previous experience I knew the rooms were only small, so he would hear everything and be a bundle of nerves in the waiting room. As I walked to the doctor's with my bump feeling heavy and ready to burst I had that feeling of impending – I wouldn't say doom because that isn't the right word – certainty, that all mums on the brink of labour must feel. There's no getting round this one, or asking someone else to do it; you just have to go through it. On the streets people were enjoying the unusual spell of Mediterranean heat; sitting outside pubs sipping pints and Pimms and going about their daily business as I went off to have my innermost parts dusted down. It's such an odd time, awaiting labour. What you are doing is so vital to the world, but you somehow feel apart from everything that's going on.

I arrived at the doctor's surgery and was instructed to lie on the bed. I fixated on a spot on the ceiling and wished for it to be over, then, after all my worry, it wasn't that bad at all! It was a little uncomfortable and I was slightly sore afterwards, but really I shouldn't have worried as much as I had about it. I walked back to the car almost jauntily. Vernon was surprised to see me back so quickly and so upbeat. Then we had a moment where we both sat wondering if labour was going to kick in immediately, but when my waters didn't break and my contractions didn't come thick and fast we drove back home. One thing that did happen was that my stomach tightened almost as soon as I left the doctor's surgery. I kept wondering if this was what a contraction was, but I knew it couldn't be

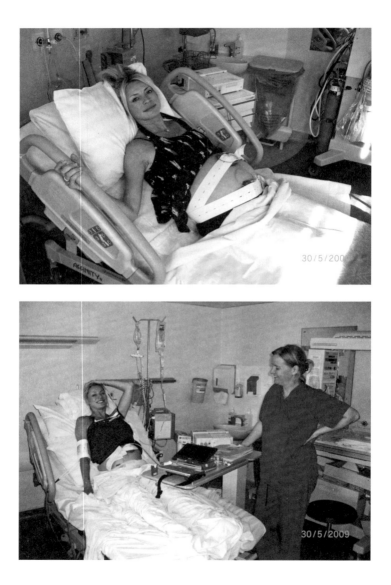

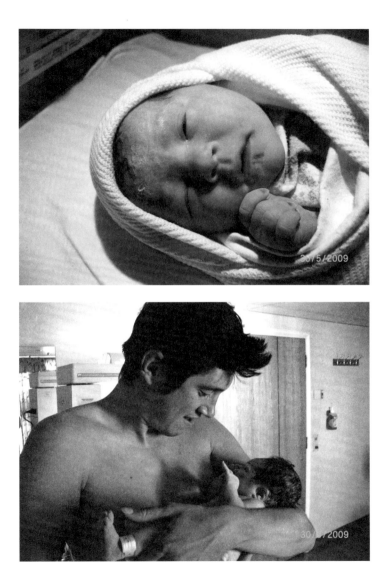

as it wasn't relaxing and contracting, it had just hardened like a medicine ball. It was as if the muscles around my stomach had tightened in preparation for what was ahead.

We went home and made sure that I had everything I needed for the hospital. My bag was already packed, but I also brought a portable DVD player and (honestly) some tea bags. I seemed to remember that last time I was in with Phoebe every cup of tea I had was weak and I can't even open my eyes in the morning without a good strong cup of tea, so there you have it, I brought my own Yorkshire Gold. Peter Kay eat your heart out. That night my mum was staying at our house in preparation for looking after Phoebe while we went into hospital. Mum was a big help and I seem to recall going to bed and sleeping quite well for someone who was anticipating a contraction any minute. The next morning we were up at six and trying to be as quiet as possible, but Phoebe was also awake, wanting to wave us off. She was as excited as anyone about the arrival of our new baby.

We arrived at the hospital and checked into the room where I would give birth to Amber. I had chosen it on a recce of the hospital a few weeks before. I know that this isn't something that is always possible in an NHS hospital, but in a lot of hospitals you can request a certain room and if it is free it will be given to you on a first-come first-served basis. One thing to remember about rooms in NHS hospitals that offer birth pools or active births, they often do not have the facilities to cater for someone requesting an epidural during labour and you cannot have an epidural if you are in the water anyway. So you will need to check with your midwife and ask them what the situation is if you are trying to make a decision about your best options for the type of birth you would, in an ideal world, like to have.

The room we were in was great. It was light and airy as it had French doors that opened out on to a small terrace looking out onto the London streets below. Vernon was familiar with the area, as it is near where he broadcasts his Radio 1 show, and the pub across the road where he and other people who work at Radio 1 sometimes go for a drink.

I hadn't eaten since midnight, in case there were complications and I needed a Caesarean, and as a result I was starving, but I had to try not to think about it. I know that if you are having a natural birth you are usually encouraged to bring in snacks to keep your energy levels up, but because of my previous Caesarean I couldn't. Believe me, I would have had a full cooked breakfast given half a chance. I can't function without my breakfast!

I was to be wired up to a CTG machine that monitors foetal distress, which is a common procedure when being induced. They prepared me for that, but I was still, for the time being, free to walk around. Then I was given a gel pessary of prostaglandin, a hormone-like substance that helps bring about contractions, and is another way of trying to induce labour before they finally go up a gear and do it chemically through a drip. It was about 8 a.m. when all of this was taking place. A few minutes later the obstetrician came in and examined me to see how I was getting on. My cervix was dilating, but not by much. It would need to be at 10cm (fully dilated) before I would have to push and I hadn't even had a contraction yet. Once she had checked me over and was satisfied that I would probably have to wait a few hours to see if the pessary had worked its magic the obstetrician said that she would leave me in the more than capable hands of the midwife.

In films and TV shows childbirth is often depicted as a mad dash to the hospital with an immediate labour that takes a few minutes. In real life there is often far more waiting around involved; even when you are in the painful throes of full-blown labour it can take some hours. Vernon was great and really supportive, he knew that when I needed leaving alone to just leave me alone. He could tell when I didn't want him standing over me. In fact, he decided that the best thing to do was to get to the shop and buy me as many magazines and sweets as he could carry. There's a man who knows how to sort me out in a crisis. So Vernon went out to get the magazines and himself some food (with strict instructions not to come back and eat it in front of me, as I was so hungry I could have gnawed at my own arm) and I sat back and waited for something to happen. By about 10.30 a.m. I began to have mild contractions. I say mild now, but at the time they felt strong until I got into the swing of it later in the day and felt the real pain of back-to-back contractions.

I got up and walked out on to the balcony. There was a hot summer haze that had settled on the city and it looked really magical from the balcony. Despite the heat, it felt light and airy from a few storeys up. I pulled up a chair and put my feet up on the balcony, enjoying the calm before the storm.

Vernon arrived back with some magazines and some contraband Tutti Fruttis, which I devoured as by this time I needed the sugar and was feeling pretty shaky. I was confident that I was going to have a natural birth. The midwife suggested at this stage that I try a dummy run with the gas and air. She told me to wait until I felt a contraction coming and then to put the tube in my mouth, bite down and inhale. At first I thought it was great. I had a really euphoric floating sensation, but after a few goes it made me feel nauseous. I knew that it didn't feel right for me and that it just wasn't going to cut it as the contractions I was feeling now were hurting and I wasn't anywhere near fully dilated.

The membrane sweep and the gel prostaglandin must have done something, as I was definitely in labour, but progress was slow. The midwife decided to get me hooked up to the drip so they could go into the next stages of labour, which was to break my waters and administer Syntocinon, a synthetic version of the hormone oxytocin. The midwife put the needle in my hand for the drip, but for some reason it refused to stay in. Every time she fixed it back in place with tape it came back out again. It was very painful and I really hate needles, but didn't want to appear a wuss so I tried my best to put a brave face on. She finally secured it after a lot of grappling, but the thought that there was a needle just sitting there in my hand made me feel slightly queasy.

Vernon was my rock, asking me every two minutes if there was anything he could do to help. He also persuaded the midwife to let me have a cup of tea – nectar when nothing but a Tutti Frutti had passed my lips for 12 hours. Vernon knew how much it meant to me to be able to give birth naturally. And kept giving me the reassurance I needed that I could do it. Meanwhile, I assured *him* that there wasn't an awful lot he could do except hold my hand, put his feet up and watch the Cup Final on the telly!

I had always said that I would have an epidural if I felt the need for one. I think that giving birth is heroic enough without putting yourself through agonizing and traumatizing pain.

I understand why women choose to avoid this level of pain relief it if at all possible. Many simply want to be fully in control of their labour and in tune with their bodies. Some midwives believe that having an epidural can extend the period you are in labour, leading to tearing or the need for an emergency Caesarean. It can also leave you with a headache for a few days after the birth. There is also the worry that an injection in your spine could cause irreparable damage and no amount of statistics telling you that it is an extremely safe form of pain relief will alleviate that concern. However, when those contractions began to build I knew that I was willing to take any help I was offered to alleviate the pain.

The anaesthetist was called and at the time Vernon was out getting food. I was worried as my previous experience of an epidural had left me bruised and sore; I just wanted to get it in my back as quickly as possible. The anaesthetist prodded around with his fingers working out the best place in the spine to put the needle. He then numbed the area with some smaller injections before making his incision with the larger epidural needle. I was bent double and wet with sweat, I was so nervous. Just as he was about to perform this delicate task my phone, which was on silent at the side of me, began to vibrate. It was Vernon calling. I tried to ignore it, but the anaesthetist seemed adamant that I answer it. 'It's your husband calling,' he informed me, reading over my shoulder. I felt like saying, 'Can you concentrate on my back please! You know, just for the next minute or so, and then feel free to look at who's calling on my phone all you want!' Argh! It was so frustrating! I didn't answer my phone and the anaesthetist did manage to complete the procedure expertly.

By the time the midwife broke my waters with something that looked a bit like a crochet hook the epidural had taken hold and I thankfully didn't experience the feeling of wetting myself, which I'd worried about and tried not to pay too much attention to the subsequent mopping up. This birth lark really is a messy business.

It was around this time that the obstetrician administered the Syntocinon. The mobile epidural was doing its job and soaking up most of the pain, but there was a little 'window' of pain that the epidural just couldn't get too. The pain that I felt there was excruciating and I cannot imagine what it would have felt like if I hadn't had pain relief. This apparently isn't uncommon and can often be fixed by changing position or having a 'top up' of epidural. With hindsight though, having that window of pain allowed me to know when my contractions were coming and when to push, so I'm actually thankful for it. I don't think I was saying that at the time though!

A couple of things that I have subsequently learned about being induced with Syntocinon is that many women describe the contractions as more painful than when they have gone through natural childbirth with no intervention. Others describe it as going from nothing to full-blown labour without the gradual build up of contraction pain that normal labour allows. It can also put the baby under stress, which is why the foetus is continually monitored.

By about half past three the obstetrician checked to see how far I was dilated: 7.5cm. Great! I thought, I'm getting there. I could tell that Vernon, who had been back for a while, was on pins. I was feeling really uncomfortable now and just wanted to hibernate and pull the blanket over my head. I told him to go to the pub over the road, which, as luck would have it, was playing the Cup Final. I knew that he didn't really want to leave me, but that part of him was relieved. I know that we women go through all the pain, but it must be really difficult for a man to stand by helpless, as you see your other half going through something so agonizing. Vernon went across to the pub and I promised we'd call him as soon as I was fully dilated and pushing.

Now that I was alone I began to want to ask lots of questions, was I doing this right? Will I know how and when to push? Was everything okay? Every time the midwife or the obstetrician looked at the monitor I watched their faces to check that they weren't worried about my baby. Suddenly I began to shake uncontrollably. The midwife reassured me that it was the shakes from the epidural, like I had experienced with Phoebe, and that it would pass; which it did, but it was still very scary nonetheless. I felt like crying, but managed to hold back, I wanted to be brave for me and for my baby.

The midwife suggested that I try to sleep. Now this might very well be possible with an epidural that has reached all the parts it was intended to, but as I was feeling the contractions, and they were only a few minutes apart, there was little chance of having 40 winks. Instead, I crawled under the blanket and tried to rest as best I could.

When the obstetrician next checked my cervix she announced, 'You're fully dilated, it's time to get Vernon back from the pub'. I had gone from 7cm to 10cm dilated in just over an hour! She calmly rang him for me, knowing that his legs would go from under him if there was any alarm in her voice, and told him it was time to come back. Vernon must have run over because he was back within minutes. I asked him to go back on the balcony. I know that a lot of women reading this will want their partners there to hold their hand and reassure them, but at the time I just wanted to know that Vernon was close by and to get on with the business of having the baby myself. Quite honestly I knew I had to push like a wild woman and get her out quickly, since if the labour was prolonged it would mean an emergency C-section. Vernon went outside and paced like a madman (he later told me) up and down the balcony.

The midwife told me it was time to push. I put my legs in the stirrups and knew that I had to concentrate every bit of will and energy I had to get this baby out safely into the world. Then something came over me and I could feel my baby ready to come into the world; it really did feel like a force of nature. I let go and shouted and screamed like a primitive woman. All I could think was that I didn't want to go through a Caesarean again and hope I could do this without tearing and needing stitches. I pushed so hard, again and again, under the instruction of the midwife and the obstetrician. I kept looking at the clock and thinking that my baby would soon be here. 'One more push,' The midwife said. It was a white lie, she said it three times. They told me that the baby's head was there and I could feel it if I wanted to. I didn't want to touch my baby until I could hold her in my arms, I just wanted her out and safe. I would push and she would inch out and go back in again. 'One more push,' the midwife said again. Stop lying! I thought, but this time she was right. With one almighty push and primal scream, Amber was here in the world.

I flopped back on to the bed, exhausted, and they lifted her out and placed her straight on my chest. Vernon was there straight away. He was mesmerized. She cried immediately, which had been something I'd panicked about with Phoebe, and it just made my whole body relax with relief. I lay there with my baby and the only way to describe the feeling was euphoric. I may have cursed the window that the epidural couldn't reach during the birth, but now I was glad of that pain. I felt that it had helped me to know when the right time to push was and had become something to work with in that last part of labour. Amber soon began suckling. She had lain for a while on me and then made her way to the breast, without having to be guided. It's so wonderful to see – in the truest sense of the word – how your baby just knows what to do.

The midwife took Amber from me and wiped her down. Vernon was talking to her and as soon as she heard his voice she turned her head towards him in recognition. We both looked at one another, it was such a special moment; she was minutes old and yet innately knew her daddy. The midwife handed Amber to Vernon and he took his top off because I'd read somewhere that it was good for dad to have skin to skin contact with the baby too, and for the little one to smell the scent of both parents as soon as possible. I don't know how much truth there is in it, but it seems to make sense and it was a lovely bonding moment.

Quite soon after that, the midwife headed over to the bed and began giving me a bed bath without being asked, which was a shock! There went my dignity again.

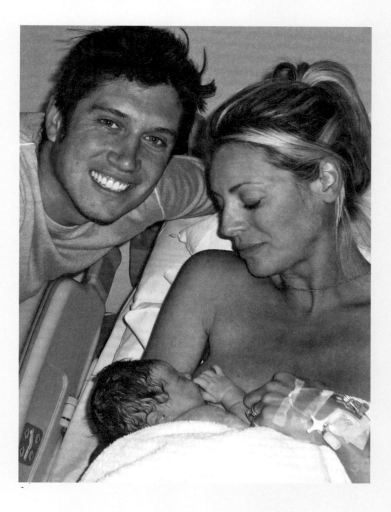

Reality
Bites

Bringing Our
Baby Home

Thinking back to those first few days with Phoebe as a newborn, the thing that I remember most is how terrified we were. Walking out of the hospital with a baby that was only a few days old was so scary. I looked down at Phoebe, so tiny in her car seat, and it suddenly struck me that Vernon and I were solely responsible for making sure she was loved, cared for and safe. The responsibility is overwhelming when it hits you. I wanted to wrap her up and hide her away from the world! Everything suddenly seemed like a danger. Even the most ordinary daily event now suddenly had potentially life-threatening consequences. I hoped that feeling this way was normal, I couldn't be this protective for ever, I'd surely drive myself and everyone else to distraction.

When we put her in the car we were so careful to make sure that she was in the car seat correctly that it took an age to get her secured. We had the added problem that there were paparazzi rumoured to be outside the front of the hospital, which really would have put the pressure on, trying to make sure our precious new baby was safely in the car while photographers snapped away. Luckily the hospital staff were really helpful and let us use their underground car park so that we could get Phoebe into the car without being photographed being clueless as to how to put a baby in a car seat.

Back at our flat Vernon carried the car seat, my baby bag, all the baby paraphernalia we had suddenly acquired and presents

3/6/2009

19/6/2009

that had been brought to the hospital up three flights of stairs. By the end of it all he was exhausted. I went into Phoebe's room and finally allowed myself to hang up the clothes that I had superstitiously hidden away until she was safely with us.

Now we were back home, other than Phoebe's room, our once cool London pad now seemed the opposite of baby friendly. The corner bath was impossible to negotiate with a sore Caesarean scar and a babe in arms, there just didn't seem to be a good angle to bathe her from. The lack of a lift was a total pain and the roof terrace just looked like a well-manicured diving board through my new-parent eyes. We had put an offer in on what would become our new home. Where once living in a family-friendly house had seemed like just an idyllic idea it now seemed like a necessity.

So here we were, back home with our baby. We fumbled our way through our first night as a family trying to be as gentle with our little one as possible, as if we were making sure we didn't break her. There was no handbook laying out a definitive guide of what to do in any eventuality, there was no dedicated hotline; we just had to get on with it.

I tried to be as gentle as possible as I pulled her little baby grow over her delicate head. The fontanelle was something I was so scared to go near for fear of hurting her. The fontanelle is the slight indent at the top of a baby's head, which is where the bones of the skull meet. They aren't joined at first so the bones can move over each other to help the head pass through the vagina during delivery. Her little arms were still rounded from months in the womb and I felt that in dressing her I might straighten them out too much and hurt her, the poor little mite.

We took her into the bathroom and gave her her second bath. I had missed her first bath in hospital since I had been confined to the bed, which I wasn't happy about, but at least Vernon had been there. This time we had her all to ourselves. We debated whether to use water or soap. Vernon was all for lathering her up, but I'd read that soap can strip babies' skin and that they should just be bathed in water. We didn't know whether to use a flannel or a sponge or just our hands. Did we wash her hair? She was so brand new, would she need her hair washing this early? These were all things I was sure I should know from the books I had read during my pregnancy, but all the information I had gathered just seemed jumbled. We just tried to be as gentle as possible. She loved the water and kept turning her head towards it appreciatively – I know she was too young at the time, but I could have sworn she smiled, and it made Vernon and I feel that we must be doing something right.

We lifted her from the bath and wrapped her in a hooded towel – I find these really handy as they cover baby's head and dry the hair without having to roughly towel dry it – and brought her into the nursery. We dried her down, put a newborn nappy on her and a tiny babygro. As we were doing this something fell from the shelf (a basket) narrowly missing Phoebe's head. I reacted as if we were in the middle of an air raid, launching myself across her. I lay there shaken, since when did baskets just leap off shelves? There were hidden dangers everywhere. Once we'd got over it we both let ourselves relax a little, sit back and just marvel at what we were seeing: there she was, our gorgeous daughter, ready for her first night at home and we'd managed to bathe her and dress her and even divert flying objects all by ourselves. It was such a small thing but it felt like a huge achievement.

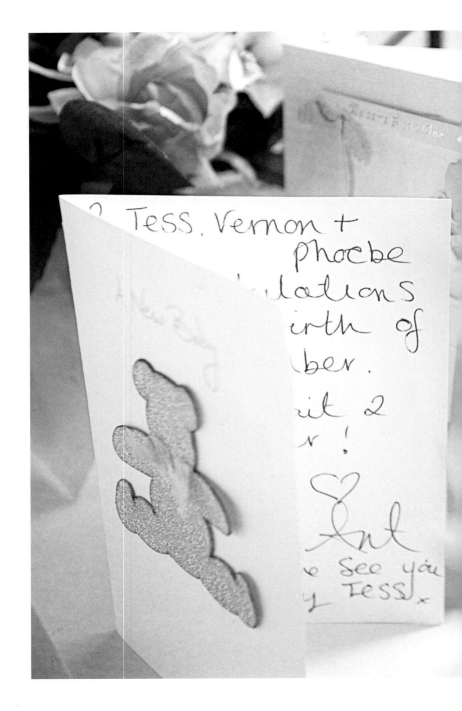

Feeding

The First Few Weeks

I gave careful consideration to breastfeeding while I was pregnant. I knew midwives recommended breastfeeding as the best possible start you could give your child, giving her antibodies and building up her immune system. From what I read, and was told, compared to breast milk, bottle milk could only ever come, at best, a close second. However, I'd just like to say at this stage that I do think there is a great deal of pressure put upon women to breastfeed. In those first few weeks after giving birth, some mums are not able to breastfeed, for physical or psychological, reasons and no one should make you feel that you have to do something that just isn't working for you. Breast might well be best, but it's hard to remember that when you're crying through the pain of cracked nipples for the fourteenth night in a row. Breastfeeding isn't easy and you do have to be shown how to do it to avoid cracked nipples!

I decided that I really wanted to give breastfeeding my best shot. I didn't really have anyone in the family to ask at that stage, as I was the only one out of me and my sister to have kids and my mum hadn't breastfed. Back in her day mums were given their babies to feed, but only allowed 15 minutes on each breast before they were taken away again. This was all in the name of building a routine, but may have meant that often the milk just dried up and the women were left with no alternative but to bottle feed. So when Phoebe was born I had to ask the midwife and the health visitor for help.

21/10/2004

The midwife showed me how to position Phoebe close to me with her head positioned so that her nose was next to my nipple. This way she would search out the nipple herself and latch on. This all sounds very easy, but at first it's a bit of a struggle. Your milk doesn't 'come in' until about the third day. Up til then you produce a thick, creamy substance called colostrum, which, although full of nutrients, doesn't do much in the way of filling your baby up. This can mean that for the first few days you are utterly convinced you are doing things wrong because your poor, brand-new baby never seems quite sated. After the third day, though, when your milk comes in, you are presented with huge blue-veined mammaries that you can't quite believe are yours!

I remember asking the midwife a number of times if I was doing things right and she would grab at my boob and manhandle it into place. It was another example of having to accept that during pregnancy, labour and the first few weeks (if not months!) of being a mum, all dignity goes out of the window. Your poor beleaguered boobs become public property. Once I thought I'd got the hang of it the health visitor came to the house and demanded that I show her that I was doing it correctly. I sheepishly got my boob out and she looked at me like I was a modern art painting that she couldn't quite decide about. I tried my best to pass the test so that she would stop staring at me and I could cover myself up again.

The pain that I felt at the beginning with both babies was intense, but with Amber it was excruciating. In fact, the pain was so bad that I nearly gave up. I would sit there with her latched on and I would dig my nails into my hands to divert the pain. I don't consider myself a wuss and a bit of pain is to be expected with breastfeeding until you get it right, but with Amber I really did have to stop myself from screaming. But it settled down with both girls after two weeks. After that I really did think that breastfeeding was a far easier option than bottle feeding.

I was very shy about breastfeeding at first and when Phoebe was born ponchos were the height of fashion, thankfully. I had a poncho for every occasion. I would hide my baby under the material and let her feed, being careful that no one caught a glimpse of skin. Vernon was working in LA when Phoebe was small so I found my poncho particularly useful for long flights, when breastfeeding is really handy for you the mum (no popped ears for baby and no bottles needing to be sterilized), but it can be a bit of an eye sore for other passengers. I did worry at first what other people thought and if I was offending them, but as time marched on I became far more laid back about breastfeeding and would have quite happily breastfeed at the top of a hill or in a Marks & Spencer café, it didn't bother me. And I think me being relaxed meant that other people didn't really notice.

One thing that I never really enjoyed about breastfeeding, although it became part and parcel of every day life, was expressing. 'Expressing' is the term used for extracting your milk from your breast using a mechanical or hand-operated pump. There's no way of dressing it up or making it sound glamorous. It is what it is, unfortunately. I hated the whirr of the machine, I hated the fact that it looked like some modern cattle farming technology. But it was a necessary annoyance when I went back to work and I had to have the pump with me all the time. Also it helped keep milk patches to a minimum. There were a number of occasions where I answered the door to a delivery man with those tell-tale nipple stains and only realized what had happened when they didn't know where to look. I also couldn't believe at first that I would start to produce milk when I was out and about if someone just mentioned Phoebe, even if she wasn't there!

One thing that I don't remember anyone telling me before I had children was that when you breastfeed you keep on producing that milk, whether your little one is there or not. And that milk has to go somewhere. So I would have to express the milk and then get rid of it; pump and dump. The ideal situation would be that I kept it to bring home for Phoebe and put it in the fridge or freezer in milk storage bags, but that wasn't always practical and anyway, once I was home, she'd simply feed as normal so I didn't need to.

I never got fully into the routine of expressing before I left for work. I would make sure that there was enough milk for Phoebe for when I wasn't there, but the thought that my breasts were filling up with no baby to need them for the rest of the day was always something that I chose to deal with as it happened. So I would find myself, breast pump in hand, at the most inopportune moments. I would be in the shower trying to wash conditioner out of my hair with one hand while working the breast pump with the other. Or in the bathroom between script meetings or dress fittings. Or under the hairdresser's cloak, shouting over the whirr of the pump as my hair was teased into place. I became a slave to that breast pump during my first pregnancy, it came everywhere with me. I would break out in a cold sweat at the thought that I might have forgotten it.

My days were fairly manageable. I had two six-hour days with show day being the only trying day when I would be away

from Phoebe from 8.30 a.m. until midnight. During these days the breast pump became my best friend. There were only so many black dresses that I could wear. Black is a bit of a no no on TV and I didn't want to look like I was dressed for a funeral for the entire series, so having the pump at hand meant that I could keep my seepage problems to a minimum – and they did happen. There were a few occasions on live TV when I would feel milk trickling down the inside of my dress. Of course I had breast pads with me, but sometimes they just weren't enough to mop up the flow. If I hadn't had the pump I would have seriously lactated all over the lovely designer frocks, not something the British Public want to sit down to on a Saturday evening, I'm sure you'll agree.

The hairiest moment I had with the breast pump and working on live TV wasn't on *Strictly*, but on a show called *Make Me a Supermodel*. My boobs felt as if they were about to burst and I was frantically trying to express in time for my cue to go on air, and this was live TV! I had mistimed the whole thing and as I stood talking to the however many millions of people who were watching I prayed that no one could tell that one boob was half the size of the other and the larger one was leaking and felt about to pop! I was mortified, and when the link finished I've never been so relieved as I ran back to my cattle machine and got at the other boob.

Around the same time the final of series two of *Strictly* was held in the Tower Ballroom in Blackpool. I stayed over for the night, which was the first time I had left Phoebe overnight. It was awful leaving her, but there was also a guilty pleasure in having my first guaranteed night's sleep. As I was away for over 24 hours I had been expressing away and had stockpiled quite a hefty amount of milk, which I had stored in the mini bar for safe keeping. It was only the day after, as I drove down the M1, that my face dropped in horror. I'd left the breast milk in the mini bar. I was mortified. Vernon thought it was hilarious though, and suggested that someone might put it on eBay. He was joking, but the thought made my toes curl!

Someone once asked me if breastfeeding was something that I had thought of in terms of what would happen to my body afterwards. I can honestly say that it was never ever an issue. Vanity never came into my decision to breastfeed and if I had considered bottle feeding as an alternative it wouldn't have been because of how it might affect my breasts. I never thought for a moment of not breastfeeding or worried about tales of people with boobs down to their knees because of breastfeeding. On the contrary, breastfeeding helped me get back in shape after both babies. I could literally feel my uterus contracting when I fed and the weight fell off me. We use up to 1,000 calories a day from breastfeeding, so no wonder.

A mistake I think that I made with Phoebe was that I breastfed to comfort her as well as to feed her. I ended up demand feeding, which was pretty exhausting. When I first tried to wean her she would search for the breast, then I would feel guilty, give in and not be able to set about the task in hand. It meant that I didn't wean her fully until she was 12 months and that she couldn't settle herself, something that I think may have contributed to her not being able to settle herself to sleep for the first couple of years.

Phoebe hasn't been at all sickly and I like to think that this is in part due to having been breastfed. When all the other children at her nursery came down with chicken pox she escaped pox free. Okay, I realize that my breast milk wasn't a vaccine for chicken pox, but I like to think it may have helped!

Breastfeeding the Second Time Around

Having breastfed Phoebe I had assumed that it wouldn't be much of a problem breastfeeding Amber. How wrong was I? For the first few days I was fairly relaxed about it. Having been there before I knew it would take a few days before my milk came in and Amber would drink the nutrient rich colustrum until then. On average, this can take between three and five days, but can be shorter or longer. It is advised that you feed your baby solely from the breast until this happens, but after three days I began to worry. Amber was hungry and I wasn't producing anything. I was letting her suckle constantly in the hope that this would kickstart some activity, but nothing happened. There was no hardening of my breasts as I'd felt the first time around, no sign that milk was going to arrive soon.

I kept looking at Amber and feeling terrible, I was starving my poor baby. I began to feel annoyed and resentful, it wasn't like I wasn't trying or wasn't willing – so where was this milk? To add insult to injury the midwife came to the house and suggested I wasn't positioning her correctly. I knew it had nothing to do with that, she could put her in any position she liked, if there wasn't any milk, it wasn't going to work. When I showed her that I knew what I was doing she backed down and admitted that yes it was strange for it to take so long, but that I should persevere.

We were back at home by now. My mum and Vernon's dad were there, we still had builders in the house and even though everyone was encouraging me to relax I couldn't; when people are in my house I feel that I have to look after them. I was running around making tea and sandwiches. Vern was trying to encourage me to sit down and take some of the burden from me, but I've never been one for just sitting down, even when I'm shattered I keep going. The whole house felt stressful and busy and looking back this atmosphere probably added to my inability to produce milk in that first week. Pretty soon my Stepford-Wife smile began to, understandably, slip.

On day four I hit rock bottom. I didn't realize that it is really common for new mums to experience the baby blues three or fours days after giving birth. I didn't know what was happening to me. Being a mum for four and a half years I was fairly used to having mini-meltdowns, but this was something different. I just didn't feel like me and although it didn't last long I can remember thinking that if I didn't get a grip I could easily slip into post-natal depression. It was such an awful way to feel and a terrible couple of days – I kept looking at Amber, this gorgeous new baby of mine and feeling like I was letting her down or was no use to her.

Vernon tried to keep my spirits up, but no matter what anyone else said, I felt terrible. I started fretting about things that had never really troubled me before. I still looked pregnant; I was convinced that I was never going to lose the baby weight and I would be left with a saggy belly down to my knees. This sounds frivolous and unfounded now looking back. I just wasn't giving myself a break, I was only just home from having a baby, what did I expect? But at the time it seemed so real and so important. Like I was losing a grip on my identity. I took to our bedroom and cried. Everything seemed too much. Childbirth is

21/10/2004

a huge strain on our bodies and yet we are constantly presented with images of women who seem to bounce back the day after. I can only imagine that they are pretending that everything is fine and that they are secretly cringing every time they go to the loo and find that their muscles haven't caught up from all the pushing and shoving they've had to do. And of course I was still feeling quite fragile due to all those breastfeeding hormones.

My desperation to breastfeed successfully was obviously affecting other people in the house. I realized this when I found Phoebe trying to breastfeed a teddy bear! 'Don't tell Daddy,' she said to me conspiratorially. I promised her that it would be our little secret. Of course it's perfectly normal for young children to copy their parents – hence the popularity of toy kitchens and dressing up toys. I even remember when I was pregnant Phoebe stuffing a pillow up her jumper as a 'baby', but it was hard not to be paranoid!

It was six long days after I had given birth to Amber that my milk finally arrived. I was sitting with Amber suckling away when I felt something and looked down, she seemed to be swallowing. I looked at my mum who dashed across the room to see what was happening. Yes, she confirmed that Amber was finally feeding from me. I felt like throwing a party. I had been just about ready to throw in the towel and bottle feed her. But my elation was to be short lived. The pain I felt was worse than childbirth; like a thousand hot needles poking into my breasts. It was pure agony. This continued for at least another week. I would sit feeding Amber and actually shout with pain. It must have been hard for Vernon and my mum to watch, but they knew that I was adamant I was going to carry on and get through it so they tried not to interfere. I wanted to do it for both Amber and for me. I was given a number for the La Leche League (their web address is www.laleche.org.uk) who offer advice on breastfeeding. They suggested it might be thrush as this is something that can occur in breastfeeding mums. But there were none of the signs. The same went for mastitis, another common complaint among new mums, but again it wasn't that.

With Phoebe, to begin with, I would wake in the night drenched in sweat with night fevers, which is something else that can happen when you are first breastfeeding. The midwife kept trying to reassure me that it would stop hurting and that we'd establish a pattern and everything would be fine. With Phoebe this had seemed like reasonable advice because she obviously knew best, but with Amber I did begin to worry. I'd done all this before and the pain hadn't been this acute or lasted for this long. I did try a few remedies. The pain was internal, so I thought that creams wouldn't help. Instead I put cabbage leaves in my bra. I was sitting around, stinking of eau d'cabbage, getting funny looks from the builders and thinking, there's no way a man would put up with this.

I'm aware that I'm not painting the most serene picture of baby suckling at mummy's breast, I'm just trying to be honest. The good news is that eventually, when Amber was two weeks old, the pain began to ease and eventually subsided altogether – when it did, it was bliss.

With Amber I am planning to wean her sooner that I did with Phoebe, but we'll see when the time comes.

Bottles and Sterilizers

Although I was breastfeeding Phoebe, I did want to get her used to a bottle so that once I was back at work, which would be in less than seven weeks, I would be able to express and leave milk for Vernon to feed her. To begin with we gave her one bottle a night. Some babies can get something called 'nipple confusion' where they take to the bottle more readily than the breast if they are offered one and then find it very difficult to be breastfed. Luckily for us we didn't really have this problem.

The sterilizer became something that terrorized me! It wasn't so much the sterilizer itself, it was easy enough to operate, but the idea that anything going in Phoebe's mouth must be spotlessly clean made me worry. I would use plastic tongs to pick things out of the sterilizer, but then if I touched the bottle or the teat I would feel the need to start the process again. I relaxed about this after a while – I had to, otherwise I would have ended up with an elaborate set-up resembling something a scientist handling uranium might use. I realized that as long as the bottle was sterilized and my hands were well washed Phoebe was probably going to be okay. Hygiene does become a big concern when you first have a baby and it can preoccupy your every move. Your baby is so tiny and her immune system so new that you feel you have to stave every germ off for her.

New Baby and Sleep

Although the nursery was all ready for Phoebe to move into, it would be a while before she would sleep in her own room. She would sleep with us in our room in her Moses basket for the next six months, or at least that was the plan. I didn't realize at the time that she would be three when she finally settled in her own room, but more of that later. One of the best things I bought for those early days was a swaddling sheet, but you can use a baby-sized blanket, shawl or sheet. It wraps tightly around your baby and keeps her from hitting herself with her newly freed arms. Phoebe found it a real comfort, I suppose it simulated the feeling of being safely held and back in the womb. This doesn't work for everyone and one mum told me that every time she swaddled her baby, no matter how expertly she did it, the baby would escape, Houdini style, leaving a pile of swaddling at his side as he lay snuffling quietly next to it as if nothing had happened.

I remember being completely paranoid about Phoebe's breathing. When she was snuffling away, making sounds like a guinea pig, I would worry it wasn't normal, that her airwaves were blocked and would move her to a different position. When she was silent I would slam all the lights on, panicking that she wasn't breathing, only to realize that she was in a deep sleep and I needn't have panicked.

I know that health professionals advise against having your baby in bed with you, but I can't think of a single mum that hasn't snuggled up with their little one next to them. That's not to say I wasn't wide awake and constantly being careful not to roll over on Phoebe, I just wanted to hold her in the bed with me. It wasn't something I made a habit of, but when she was crying for the third or fourth time on the same night I just surrendered and put her in our bed.

The other sleep worry I had was whether I had the room at the right temperature and Phoebe suitably clothed. I didn't come across Grobags (a baby sleeping bag) until she was six months old. Up to then I would put her in a babygro, worry about whether it should be long sleeved or short sleeved and put a blanket over her – it is recommended that babies under 12 months do not have duvets. Every night I would worry. Am I wrapping her up too much? Or too little? I would always make sure that her feet were at the bottom of the Moses basket, as this is the recommended way for newborn babies to sleep. This is because babies don't know how to free themselves once they have shuffled under a blanket, which is why the sleeping bags are such a great idea as it isn't instinctive to push the clothing off. This really worried me and I would constantly check to make sure she was sleeping at the bottom of the basket and that the covers were small enough that they only covered her and she wasn't at risk of getting stuck under them.

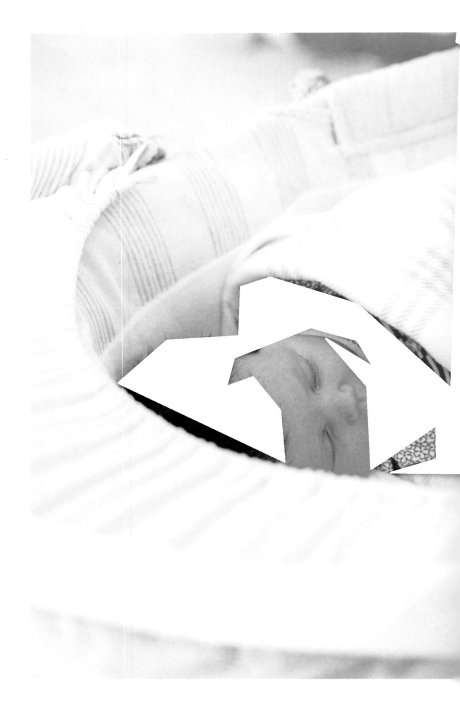

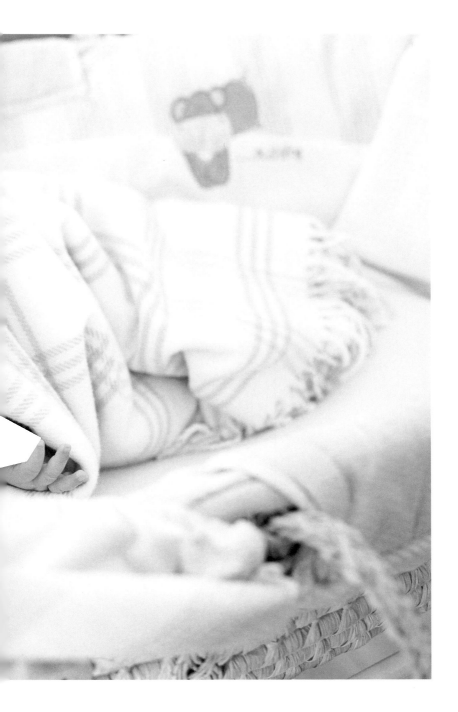

Taking Your Baby Out and About for the First Time

There is nothing quite like the first time you wrap your baby up, put them in the pram and take them out into the big wide world on your own. Not with your mum, not with your other half: just you and your baby. I think the first time I went out with Phoebe on my own was one of the most daunting things I had ever done. Having been out a few times with Phoebe in the pram with Vernon or his mum or my mum, and having managed to leave the flat on my own with Phoebe once or twice, I felt that I was getting on top of this being a mum business.

One day, Vernon went to work without assembling the pram, which was something he was really good at and something I found totally baffling. He showed me how to do it before he left, we had a run through and I thought that I'd manage to assemble it on my own, but I obviously hadn't quite got the hang of it. Now I don't want to come across as a weak and feeble female here, because I'm not, but when you first get a pram (especially a 'travel system' where there are lots of bits to slot in for different occasions) you can feel that you need an engineering degree to set it up. I was in a rush as I had to be at the doctor's for 11 o'clock. I had managed to dress Phoebe and get her ready for the cold October day, but I was looking a bit of a state. I had dripping wet hair, no make-up on, and I found myself out on the street having left my poor baby three flights up in the flat in her Moses basket as I went at piecing the pram together – I'd have had more luck trying to finish a Rubik's cube.

As I struggled, I didn't realize there were two paparazzi taking pictures of me. They had a white van by our house with the rear doors open and a pile of crisp boxes in the back to make it look like they were delivery men. They had cut a hole out of one and put a camera through it. I was losing the plot as it was and it was a good job I didn't know they were there. I didn't find out about it until over a year later when a friend of mine rang to say she'd been watching a programme about paparazzi and had seen the pictures of me struggling with an explanation of how the pictures had been acquired.

I finally pieced the pram together and ran up to Phoebe, my heart thumping, feeling like a bad mum at having left her out of my sight. I ran back down the stairs with her in my arms, hoping no one had stolen the pram and raced her around to the practice for the check up.

I managed to get to the surgery on time, feeling as if I'd run a marathon. I was shaking as I arrived through the doors. As I settled myself in the waiting room, with Phoebe in my arms, I looked around the room. There were other mums there with babies who looked to be a similar age to Phoebe. I may have been imaging it, but they all looked coiffed and serene, whereas I felt bedraggled and hyper. How did they do it? I wondered. Would I ever be able to leave the house without the assembly of the pram making me want to cry, and without feeling the need to pack everything Phoebe owned to come with us on our short journey? I didn't feel the low that I would feel years later with Amber when my milk didn't come, I just felt like everything was a Herculean effort.

Once I left the doctors' I was so pleased with myself that I treated myself to a latte at a local café. Going from feeling that I couldn't leave the house to having completed my little mission successfully was so fulfilling. I felt so pleased to have overcome another mini hurdle that I could have run up to strangers in the street and shared my good news with them. It was such a small thing, but seemed so significant. I might have brought on a cold by venturing out with wet hair, but I didn't care. I was sitting here with my baby, having got to the doctors' on time, and I was now enjoying a coffee.

What to Take with You

Packing everything up in order to leave the house with a baby, even if it's just to go to the park, is often a feat of memory and dexterity. At first you feel as though you have to bring everything, including the kitchen sink, just in case … and wonder how you're going to get out of the house with anything less than a Mary Poppins-type magic bag.

Baby bags come in all shapes, sizes and colours and some have a dizzying array of compartments. Some have fold-out nappy mats, bottle warmers and mobile phone compartments. When I was younger I'm quite sure that my mum just put anything she needed for me and my sister as babies in a shopping bag or a carrier bag, but thankfully now new mums can go out with a little more style. Boots do a number of bags including a 'man bag', just in case your other half wants to take the bag with him but feels a bit silly carrying a huge bag with an Orla Kiely leaf print emblazoned across the front. There is an Australian company called Oioi that do very stylish and unobtrusive bags that have a small changing mat, bottle warmers and enough compartments so that you can separate out your baby's stuff without feeling like you're carrying around a filing cabinet. Mamas & Papas also do a very cool range of baby bags.

I had a denim Skip Hop bag with Phoebe and I loved it. It was really handy and fitted perfectly over the buggy handles. Also it was just the right size and wasn't too baffling when you looked inside it. I would pack a couple of nappies, some baby wipes, nappy sacks, a bib, a babygro (in case of throwing up) a spare bottle and a carton of milk (when Phoebe was older) and some sanitizer hand gel, as you never know where you might end up changing a nappy. I would also try to throw my own things in this bag, lip gloss, keys, purse, etc. It's cumbersome enough having to leave the house with a bag full of your baby's essentials without dragging a handbag around too.

Using a Dummy

Phoebe didn't have a dummy. At the time health professionals were recommending that babies didn't have dummies. It was suggested that they could interfere with the process of breastfeeding in the first few weeks and then later on it could cause speech impediments, although there doesn't appear to be any evidence for this.

Since then the advice has changed completely. It is now thought that dummies can dramatically reduce the risk of cot death. So with Amber we have been using a dummy. I do find it handy for when she is a bit grizzly and isn't settling, but the definite downside is that when she spits it out at night it

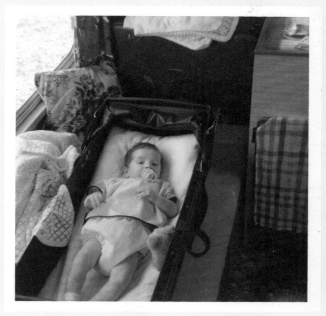

Vernon as a baby – nice outfit!

unsettles her and we have to hunt around in the Moses basket
for it and pop it back in. The general advice is to try to wean
babies off their dummy before they begin to speak, so that
it doesn't get in the way of their speech development, but
I know some people wean off earlier to make the process easier.
This makes sense, as removing a dummy from a six-month-
old is bound to be easier than battling with a two-year-old.
However, I will see how we feel about this nearer the time
as these things often stand to reason in theory, but are far
harder to carry out in practice!

Outside Help

Our parents lived so far away that it wasn't feasible or fair to ask them to take up childcare. So we contacted a nanny agency where we live and asked for a night nurse to come and look after Phoebe three nights a week for the three weeks leading up to me going back to work. I was finding the anxiety of waiting for the baby to wake up and anticipating not sleeping was actually worse than not sleeping itself. I knew if I kept on this way, and then went back to work having done a night shift the night before, I couldn't guarantee I'd be able to put one foot in front of the other, let alone string sentences together on live TV.

In getting a night nurse our hope was that she would establish a routine we could then stick to and we could take over ourselves. So for the next few weeks we had a night nurse arrive at the house at Phoebe's last feed and take her to bed, armed with bottles of expressed milk should she wake up. Just having those three nights a week of guaranteed sleep meant I could calmly focus on going back to work.

The next nanny we had was to look after Phoebe when I was at work, she would be at our house three days a week and one night for the time I was back at work. I really struggle with the idea of having someone in the house performing childcare duties when I'm there. What's the point in me if I just ship someone else in? Maybe it's just my working-class background coming through, but I just wouldn't be comfortable with it. There's also the fact that I didn't want to miss anything. Everything is a first with a baby, and every first is special. I didn't want someone else to be there for her the first time she rolled over, or crawled or walked. I wanted to be there if at all possible. So we hired the lady specifically for the days that I was working. When she first arrived she reminded me of a real-life Mary Poppins. She was a more mature lady who had her own older children and such a reassuring air about her that I wanted her to look after me as well! She made herself at home and made me a cup of tea. This small kindness made me teary, I was so grateful. Even though I was adamant that she was only there to look after Phoebe, she was so kind to me in the time that we overlapped that I felt nurtured by her too. It was such a lovely feeling, after being so tired for the past few months.

She had some old-fashioned methods that I found a real comfort and I had no problem, other than the normal guilt, in leaving Phoebe with her. She would bundle Phoebe up tightly in lots of layers and put her outside in the fresh winter air. Something that, if I'd done myself, I would have fretted about. She would sing lullabies around the house, soothing Phoebe to sleep this way. She worked with us for six months, intermittently after I finished *Strictly* because I work freelance and can often be asked to do a job at short notice (a voice over for example) and need to arrange childcare fast. But these type of jobs only last for a day and I needed someone to be as flexible as possible. This is why the agency suited us perfectly at that time.

Our mums came down as often as possible, but I always wanted them to enjoy their time with Phoebe rather than feel they were there to look after her. They were always more than willing to help out and that was something that Vernon and I were really grateful for. It is hard at times having our families so far away, but it meant when they did visit they would stay over and Phoebe would get to spend good quality time with them.

Vernon and his dad

When Phoebe was nine months old she went to nursery for two mornings a week. She was looked after by Sheena, a lovely Scottish lady, in her home and to this day we are still friends. I suppose she was more of a childminder, but it felt like a small nursery and just a warm and inviting place. This again was another step on the ladder of mum-guilt. I didn't know if we were doing the right thing, would she be well looked after? Would there be other children that demanded attention and she might get forgotten? Or, the flip side, will she like it so much at nursery that she'll think that being with her mum and dad is a bit of a let down? I know all of these feelings are irrational, but they raced through my mind as we planned for Phoebe's first day at nursery.

I needn't have worried. Phoebe loved nursery and it quickly became clear she was flourishing in this environment. It would seem that every day she would come home having learned something new. Not land mark things that made me think I was missing out on important bits of her life, but just picking up things that made me realize how quickly she was learning and growing. When she was two she moved to another nursery and was there three mornings a week, but it was still small enough so that I didn't feel like she might be lost in there. And I couldn't wait to collect her, hear about her day and scoop her up in my arms.

Baby Blues

Thankfully I have never suffered from post-natal depression. And having had the baby blues for a few days I can only imagine how awful it must be to feel so bad when everyone around you is assuming you must be ecstatic because of your new baby. I did, however, have a number of mini-meltdowns, where everything got on top of me and I would feel that I wasn't coping as well as I should have. This was often because I was putting too much pressure on myself to be a great mum: breastfeeding; doing the shopping; the cooking; the housework; and working at the same time. I struggled to hand over responsibility for things to other people. In my harder moments on myself I look at my mum and think she didn't need a team of nannies looking after me and my sister and she never had a nervous breakdown. But I know that accepting help and letting the pots pile up on the side of the sink once in a while, or guests make their own cup of tea, isn't the end of the world; I just struggled with it.

As I mentioned earlier, I really struggled at around day four with Amber. I hadn't realized that having baby blues at this time was so common, and as a result I felt as if I was going slightly mad. Basically, baby blues is caused by a combination of massively changing hormones after the pregnancy and birth, sleep deprivation and the huge psychological change of having a child. I was so low and felt that nothing I did was going to be good enough; I was a mum who couldn't even provide milk for her child. All of these thoughts were irrational and exacerbated through tiredness, but that doesn't make them any less real or scary at the time. At least with Amber I could reason with myself and think, you've done this before, you just need to take each day at a time and things will get better. However, when I had Phoebe and I had my first crisis of confidence, which I've already mentioned, I didn't know what was happening – I felt hopeless. Just the fact that you have to leave the house alone for the first time with your precious bundle is so daunting.

Another low point was driving the three and a half hour journey from our house to my mum's, alone in the car, with Phoebe. She began crying as soon as we got on the M1 and became absolutely inconsolable. I had a rear-view mirror that was positioned on the windscreen so that I could check that she was okay, but almost as soon as she started crying the mirror fell off into the passenger foot-well and I couldn't reach it. There wasn't a services for over 20 miles and I couldn't pull onto the hard shoulder because I had read the fact that it is statistically the most dangerous place to be in the UK floating around in my head, so we had to plough on. She screamed all the way to the services and I was driven to distraction, but at the same time I felt absolutely terrible. I pulled over and took her out of the car seat into my arms and she began to calm down to a whimper. Soon she was happily snuggled against me. It seemed that all she had wanted was a cuddle and a bit of attention. And there I was worried sick that something was really troubling her!

The highs and lows of being a mum can be this simple – the horrible 'I'm-not-coping' lows are counterbalanced by the amazing highs that you get from being a mum. They'd have to be otherwise no one would ever become one! And these highs didn't just come about from things I'd achieved in learning to be a mum. As each day went by it seemed that Phoebe's interest in the world was growing. And every week, if not day, seemed to present another small, but significant, milestone. From following my finger with her gaze or focusing intently on my face, to rolling over for the first time, and all that came in between, there always seemed to be something new and exciting for her to discover and that made it all feel worthwhile.

Vernon was really supportive during our time finding our feet as new parents and knew that, when I was tired, if he came home with cakes it might not make me less tired, but would certainly cheer me up! He would also encourage me to step away from the to-do list and go and have my nails done or have a massage. It wasn't something I did every week, it was just an occasional treat, but it meant that I came back feeling refreshed and happy. I suppose he was giving me permission to go easy on myself. He was also good at making sure that we had some time together and would book a baby sitter and take me out to dinner. It is great to have a husband who knows me well enough to know when I need some help and support or just some time out.

When I think about what made me feel low, other than hormones, I suppose it was the idea that I wasn't coping, rather than the reality of not coping. I think that, practically, I did quite well looking back now, but I gave myself a hard time when I was struggling. Also, I think that it is such a shock going from looking after yourself to looking after another little person. There doesn't seem to be any time alone. Not that I was looking to enrol on a pottery course or dash off on holiday, I just mean five minutes to catch up on emails or leaf through a magazine. The odd thing is, now that I'm a mum to a young baby again, I realize that there was time if I had wanted it. Newborn babies sleep a lot, but I just felt every moment I had with Phoebe when she was awake I had to be with her, and when she was asleep I should be doing something useful. Sitting on my bum, leafing through *Vogue* would have just made me feel guilty. And I haven't changed my opinion about that, I would still feel guilty taking naps and having little moments of 'me' time during the day. It's the sort of advice that I'd give to someone else, but never be able to take myself.

For the first few months I felt as though I spent most of it learning not only how to be a mum, but to manage my time and to try to loosen up a little and not battle with myself so much. I would find myself halfway through doing something, Phoebe would be asleep in her cot and then all of a sudden I'd be sobbing on the settee, feeling like I couldn't keep up with my own standards of excellence. It wasn't as if anyone else cared if my fridge was clean or the tops of doors were harbouring some dust that I hadn't seen off. Vernon would gently talk me around, telling me that I was doing a fantastic job and I didn't need to put so much pressure on myself. I knew that all Phoebe needed was to be fed and loved and that bit came easy to me, I adored her, but it was trying to relax around everything else I saw as my role that I found more difficult. Even now I run around trying to tidy up and I can't say that I've ever really managed to fully relax about it. I still run around the house cleaning up and stockpiling the fridge until it's bursting and I feed everyone who walks through my door. But as Phoebe got a little bit older, and I got more used to be being a mum and how that worked, I felt like I regained a bit of the old me and that didn't mean letting other people do things for me, but it did mean doing lots of things on the go and at once.

Going Back to Work

As I've touched on when talking about childcare, I was dreading leaving Phoebe, especially as she was only seven weeks old. I had to bargain with myself constantly: she's with her dad, he's fantastic and she won't even miss me. I only work three or four days a week and it's only for a few weeks; then I can spend all my time with her … I love my work and feel that working in a job that makes me so happy makes me a better mum and role model.

For every argument I had there was a counter argument nagging away at me, making me feel terrible, telling me I should be there 24/7 until Phoebe finally left home, whenever that might be. Every working mum I've spoken to feels this way. But a mum I was speaking to recently who stays at home and on the surface seems to have it all, told me that she is crawling the walls and would love to be out working or doing something that at least means that she could spend some of her days with adults. As much as we try to have it all, we can't, and being a mum boils down to a fine balancing act: keeping your children happy; earning money; and trying to be a good role model for your children in the best way you know how. For me that meant returning to work. I loved my job and I felt so privileged to have such a great show to be working, and that once finished, I could spend a good proportion of my time with my baby.

Phoebe was seven weeks old when I returned to the show. That year we had aired the first series in the spring and as it had been a success the BBC decided to bring it back to fit into the busy autumn/winter schedule. This meant I was back in front of the camera not long after giving birth. That first day back,

I was very wobbly. Any mention of my baby and I would start to lactate. I called home at every available opportunity and felt guilty about leaving her. At the same time I really enjoyed being in the company of adults and having grown-up conversations and that took my focus away from home. I had to be on the ball for the live show They don't call it baby brain for nothing. I had found myself peering into the fridge on a number of occasions and wondering what on earth I was looking for, before remembering that I was actually meant to be on the way to the post office and that the salad drawer was no place for the gas bill.

I was shattered, as every new mum is, but I knew that I had to keep on top of things. No one wants to see a bedraggled, half-asleep TV presenter so I kept my energy up by eating often. Not even 'little and often' just often. Bruce would joke that they had to hide the cakes and sandwiches anytime I was around as I might steel them off his plate. And I would always have a Mars Bar secreted somewhere about my person, just to be on the safe side.

Sometimes, on show day, I would bolt my lunch and then use the 20 minutes I had left to lie down. I would never sleep because I just can't during the day, but I would just rest and store my energy reserves for when it would be needed later on.

I had mum guilt throughout the day. Vernon did his radio show until lunchtime on a Saturday, but then would be back to look after Phoebe after one. I would call him and if I heard her crying I would feel terrible and helpless to do anything. Vernon would reassure me that he was more than capable and he really enjoyed having that one-on-one time with Phoebe so I would be back feeling okay again, enjoying the chance to be at work and trying not to worry. I had nothing to worry about really. Vern loved being with Phoebe and was always very hands on.

Then we would record two live shows. The adrenalin rush of this is exhilarating, but means that once the show is over all of the natural tiredness that I should have been feeling would come crashing in. I would get home at about 1 a.m. and crawl into bed. I would then be up to breastfeed in the night and the following day I would feel as if I had done ten rounds with Mike Tyson, but I would make sure I was up and out of bed spending time with Phoebe to make up for having missed her the previous day. There was no opportunity to stay in bed either, as Vernon was working on Sunday mornings then. Not that I wanted to, no matter how tired I was I wanted to be up and with Phoebe. I didn't want to miss anytime with her when I was physically there. Sundays have always been a special time for us as a family. After Vernon finished his radio show on Sunday mornings, he would come home and we'd hang out and cook a big roast at the end of the day.

I really loved being a mum but I was glad to be able to return to a job that I loved. I genuinely think that having a career that I enjoy brings out the best in me and ultimately makes me a better mum.

Six
Months
Onwards

I Really am a Mum!

When I first had Phoebe I would spend my time wondering
how other mums managed to cope, and I was told by a few
seasoned mothers that there would be a day when it would
all slot into place. For me that had definitely happened around
the six-month mark. Vern and I didn't wake up one morning and
suddenly know we had mastered things and that we could just
kick back and congratulate ourselves, far from it. It was gradual,
but lots of things happened in a short space of time that meant
I could say I was happy and confident in being a mum; we
became used to being parents, to packing a day bag for Phoebe
rather than remembering a time when it had been so easy
to just have to think about getting ourselves out of the door.
Feeding became easier. Bottles could be washed and I didn't feel
beholden to the sterilizer. When Phoebe was around six months
old she had begun to eat solids so I didn't have to feed her every
three to four hours. I was more confident in my abilities as a
mum and Phoebe was becoming more interested in everything
around her, which meant that she was easy to entertain.

We had had a number of 'firsts' that we'd managed to
overcome without too much trouble; including going on holiday,
visiting friends and going back to work. I wasn't feeling under
hormone arrest quite so much as I had in the early days and
I could get out and about freely with Phoebe in tow, rather than
sitting at home wondering if I'd ever be able to hit the sales
again. Things stopped being an effort or a hurdle to overcome,
they were now second nature. I began to actually feel sorry for
my friends who didn't have children instead of envying the

freedom they had. I had this brilliant little person here with me all the time and looking after her didn't feel like something I was learning to do any more, but something I did. I think that probably one of the biggest myths about becoming a parent is that as soon as you are handed your baby you will instinctively know what to do. You may instinctively know how to feed and love your baby, but it's hardly part of our DNA to be able to assemble a pram that comes in three parts or negotiate the tube with a sleeping baby. There is a lot to learn when becoming a mum. As Phoebe approached the six-month mark I was starting to realize that I may never know everything, but I was quickly picking things up.

Going on Holiday with a Baby

Flying

I have travelled a lot with my career and been on more planes than I care to remember. I used to pride myself on a certain efficiency where airports were concerned. I knew which queue to get in to get to the check-in desks quickly. I knew how to navigate my way around most airports with little hassle and how to make sure that in flight I got enough water down me and moisturizer on my face not to look like a dried-up prune on disembarkation. I packed carefully and even tried, on occasion, to master the capsule wardrobe that you always seem to be reading about in magazines (they never work in practice): one vest, one dress and a pair of jeans for a long weekend, slightly ambitious under-packing I think.

So when I was pregnant I naively hoped that I'd be able to take some of this travel savvy and apply it to my soon-to-be new status as a mum. I had obviously not thought that there were a few simple truths about travelling with a baby. Firstly, they come with more paraphernalia than your average packhorse. It makes gliding around duty free trying out Juicy Tubes or having a leisurely coffee as I waited for the gate number to be announced a definite thing of the past. Secondly, people seize up when they see a mother and baby about to board a plane. You can see their faces drop, it's like Russian Roulette, who's going to have the unlucky ticket that means they'll be sitting next to the potential crying machine.

Before I had children it was always the parents who were relaxed with their children, but also mindful of other passengers, who I admired. The ones who got on and let their little ankle biters scream the place down or run riot were the ones who garnered little sympathy, and drew filthy looks, from other passengers. So when I first braved a flight with Phoebe I hoped that we would be more like the former type of parent rather than the latter.

Vernon was back working in LA and we were flying to the West Coast. At the time Phoebe was almost six months. The flight was 11 hours long and I was dreading it. Not because Phoebe was particularly vocal, but because there was no way of predicting how she would react to this strange environment.

At least we were all travelling together; strength in numbers, I can't imagine doing this first long-haul journey alone. I had realized, as I'd begun to pack, that I was going to have to condense my own packing in order to fit everything of Phoebe's in. Gone were the usual five pairs of shoes. I took the pair on my feet and packed a pair of sandals and a pair of heels. I also tried to pare down the clothes I took. I packed a couple of kaftans that could be worn over a bikini for when you're still feeling self-conscious about your baby belly; Heidi Klein does really nice ones, but they can be quite expensive, so Warehouse provide a more affordable alternative. They are also good for breastfeeding when out and about. I tried to pack for the sun and worry about freak monsoon weather when I got there, should it occur. I brought sunscreen in the highest factor I could find for Phoebe and got her a sun hat and some clothes that would mean she was cool, but covered.

We had brought with us the Maclaren buggy for its first

outing. I had checked out its weight, amongst other factors, and it seemed like the most compact and lightweight option for our needs. However, the woman behind the desk had different ideas and tried to get us to put the buggy in the hold. It was going to be a bit of a struggle carrying a small baby and all our hand luggage around the airport before we got to the gate. Although Vern was willing to give it a go, I asked the woman if there was any chance we could wheel the pram to the departure gate. This was four years ago and nowadays this seems to be more common practice, but at the time the check-in assistant didn't seem too happy. It really does make life easier being able to drop your pram off at the entrance to the plane and be able to pick it up again afterwards. Eventually the check-in woman relented. One thing I would say when travelling with a small child is that on the whole people are friendly and accommodating, but if you come up against resistance about something that would really make your life easier, don't cower away just because you have a babe in arms and don't want to trouble anyone. Be as polite and firm as you would be if you were travelling alone and needed some help and more often than not people will bend over backwards.

Thanks to Vernon's work we were lucky and travelled business class on this particular flight, but it also meant we got more dirty looks than we might normally have received. I held Phoebe close to me and tried to smile at everyone who was on the plane while simultaneously conveying a soothing air that suggested I knew exactly what I was doing and that Phoebe wouldn't make a peep throughout the flight. I also vowed that as soon as she got grumpy I would feed her and then work things out from there.

When booking the flight we had been hoping to sit in the part of the plane that has a bassinette (a small, pull-down baby basket), but these seats had been taken. This was a bit disappointing, as at the time you couldn't book this seat and could only request it and hope for the best. Now, however, with most airlines you can reserve these seats when you book the flight. So we tried to make ourselves comfortable in the seats we had. After a few minutes, we discovered that the seats went flat, so we could at least take it in turns to sit with Phoebe as she lay and played or slept between our legs.

Lots of mums had whispered to me about giving her something to 'help her sleep' on the flight. But it didn't feel right giving her some sort of medication when she wasn't actually poorly, just to make her sleep. Plus I'd read that medical professionals strongly advise against it. Instead, when she was grizzly I just stuck her under my pashmina and onto my boob. I also took a bottle just in case – at this time I had begun to introduce the occasional bit of formula milk.

Babies' ears can pop on planes, like anyone else's, but it is painful and something they obviously can't communicate. The best way to avoid this is to give them a drink or a dummy, if you are using one, so that they are sucking something when the plane takes off. This alleviates the build up of pressure in the ears. With regards to bottle feeding, I found that the little cartons of SMA were a godsend when travelling. They don't need warming up and can be put straight into the bottle. Baby milk allowances are different to the 100ml fluid allowance for hand luggage, you can take more, but you may be asked to try it at the security desk. Another thing when travelling, if you are bottle feeding try not to be tempted to bring six bottles, bottle warmers and the sterilizer with you. Unless you're going somewhere ultra remote you will be able to buy bottles when you get there and you can use sterilizing tablets or even buy a portable sterilizer.

I try to travel as light as possible without forgoing any essentials. I just think there's so much to pack and remember when you have a baby with you that streamlining your packing helps to avoid being weighed down at the airport like a packhorse. I try to take as much as I can in miniature bottles and not over do it with the clothes, even children's clothes. It is tempting to pack hundreds of babygros and baby outfits, as they do tend to get through them, but I bring some hand-wash powder with me and wash things through so that I'm not trailing the girls' entire wardrobe on a plane every time we go on holiday. I also try to bring a couple of things that remind them of home. A special toy or a Grobag that they're used to sleeping in should do it. And one last thing that came in really handy was a strap-on high chair that I found. I can't remember what make it was now, but it was so handy and meant that we could feed Phoebe anywhere without having to worry whether they would have a free high chair or not.

Now back to the flight. After my initial worries and my imagination running riot making me think that we would spend the entire flight walking Phoebe up and down while she cried at the top of her lungs and we apologized, the flight went quite well. We had our normal ups and downs that we'd have in any 11-hour period, but I just hid her under my pashmina and she suckled away, so all in all our first long haul flight was fairly uncomplicated.

Being on Holiday

Once in LA, Vern had to go straight to work and begin filming. He was working on a live show so had to have his wits about him, which meant that I was on night duty – this made perfect sense to me. There's no way he'd expect me to get up when I had to work and he was off. Phoebe was only five months at the time and I did wonder, with her body clock not quite adjusted to the world yet anyway, if she could suffer from jet lag. What a silly thing to think – of course she could. And she did! Every morning for the two weeks we were there she woke at four. I would creep out of bed trying not to disturb Vern, bumping around in the dark towards Phoebe's travel cot. I would get her up, change her, feed her and dress her, put her in the pram and make my way out on to Venice Beach. By the time we had made our way there it would be five in the morning and still dark. I would walk along the sea front from Santa Monica to Venice Beach until the sun came up and I'd set up a towel on the beach and sit and look at Phoebe, making sure to keep the sand out of her eyes, and watch the ocean crashing on the shore. It was so peaceful and such a different way of looking at the world.

Before you become a mum you might see four o'clock in the morning because you've stayed up carousing for too long. Once you are a mum four o'clock can often become the start of the day – it's quite a sea change. We were the only people out in Venice at this time it always seemed; actually that's not strictly true, it was me, Phoebe and the local homeless people. I was on nodding terms with them by the time we neared the end of our holiday. We would sit on the beach until seven in the morning when the beach front stalls began opening, the groans of pain started emanating from the muscle beach and the joggers hit the pier. I would then bundle Phoebe back up, buy bagels for breakfast and head back to the apartment as Vernon was just waking up. Don't worry, it's not a one-way street and when I'm working and Vernon is off he's the one up looking after the girls and doing the bagel run! Each evening I would get Phoebe to bed, run some errands make some calls and then we'd crash in front of the TV. I'm sure that everyone back home thought we were having a glamorous old time of it in LA. If only they could have seen us.

Although I felt quite mad and sleep deprived, at the same time I knew what a unique experience this was to be having with my baby and something that I'd look back on and remember fondly. When Vernon had some rare time off we would make the most of it and head out into Hollywood and do all the touristy things. We have a picture of Phoebe underneath the Hollywood sign and by Mann's Theatre. We drove up and around Mulholland and looked out over the twinkly lights of the city, pointing at them for Phoebe who was mesmerized by them.

After this trip we felt quite brave and began to venture abroad whenever we had the opportunity. We went to Ibiza with friends, but it was one of the hottest summers there on record. The heat was unbearable for a little baby and we found it quite stressful trying to keep Phoebe out of the sun and cooled down. I don't think it helped that Vern and I were the only ones with a child. Everyone else was out partying and clubbing until the early hours and I was getting up when they were going to bed.

We have since been very adventurous and travelled to New Zealand a few times to see my sister. I think that once we'd done one trip, subsequent trips became far easier. I learned what I

Mum, me and the donkeys in Blackpool

Me and my cousins, Nicola and Stephen, on holiday on the Isle of Wight

needed to bring and what I didn't and I got more confident in myself and Vernon and Phoebe and how we travelled together as a family. I also think I relaxed a bit and stopped worrying quite so much about what everyone else thought. I think it's good to be mindful that there are other passengers around, but I don't feel the need to apologize before the girls have even made a noise anymore.

We haven't actually been abroad with both Amber and Phoebe. As I'm writing this we've just returned from a week in Cornwall, which was great and lovely to go on holiday as a family. Especially on a holiday that reminded me of the sort I used to go on as a child. We stayed in a lovely self-catering place that I found on www.babyfriendlyboltholes.co.uk. This website was a revelation; you put in your criteria and it finds somewhere baby friendly for you to stay. All of the places on the website are geared towards families, but are as far away from the holiday camp type holiday as you can imagine. They have spa retreats, luxury cottages, palatial farm houses and they seem to realize that there is more to being a baby friendly place than throwing a cot in one of the bedrooms. We ended up in Cornwall because I had forgotten to get Amber's passport in time to go abroad. Until a few years ago children could be added to their parents' passports, but now each child must have their own. A first child passport costs £46 for standard service; I've since learned that you can pay £81 for the one-week Fast Track service, which meant we could have been somewhere more exotic than Cornwall for our only week away this year, but never mind, we had a great time.

The weather might be far from guaranteed, but holidaying in this country with children is great for a number of reasons.

Firstly, you can pack everything up in the car and just go without having to decant everything you might take in your hand luggage into 100ml bottles and squeeze it all into a sandwich bag. Secondly, kids don't really care where they are. A pool in South End and a pool in Mauritius might be two very different things to us adults, but to kids it's just a pool. As long as they have somewhere to play they are pretty easy to cater for. Thirdly, you can forget half of what you meant to bring and just pick it up at a supermarket on the way. Fourthly, it is cheaper. As I write this the euro is making the pound look like the rupee so it works out far cheaper to stay at home than abroad.

Occupying Children when Travelling

I'm reminded, now that I have a baby again, that when Phoebe was little finding ways to occupy her wasn't hard, I didn't think that at the time though; I was too busy trying to get the hang of being a mum, not sleeping and worrying about this little bundle to think that tiny babies are actually quite manageable. That is said with hindsight of course and it's all very well saying this, but I know it only applies once you know what you're doing! So now, when I set off on a journey with Phoebe and Amber, I know that as long as I have milk, which obviously I do, a change of nappy for Amber and maybe a little toy to hang from her car seat, she'll be happy. Phoebe is old enough now to occupy herself happily if she wants to, and can sit for hours colouring, drawing or reading. So at the moment I'm having quite a blissful time of it where child-distracting techniques are concerned. However, with Amber I know that this is the calm before the storm and that from six months until maybe about three years I will need to remember

Vernon and his little brother Steven (love that hat!)

Vernon and Steven on holiday

what tricks of the trade I used to keep Phoebe quiet when we were out and about.

When we were travelling anywhere I used to rely on the car engine to, if not put her to sleep, at least calm her and allow her to look out of the window. There isn't a lot you can do when you're on a one-parent drive halfway across the country with a little one that has a few minutes' attention span. Phoebe was usually quite good on car journeys, but when she decided to cry she could really let rip – like the time I mentioned when I first I travelled with her alone up to my mum's.

As Phoebe got a little older, maybe 18 months onwards, she began to recognize songs that she liked so I would have CDs in the car with different sing-along songs on. These are great for keeping your little one entertained, but not so great for your sanity. I have also been known to be driving along, wondering how I'm going to calm my screaming child when another rendition of 'The Wheels on the Bus' just won't cut the mustard, and remembering that Vernon is due on the radio. I know this isn't exactly something that everyone can do, but it worked a treat for Phoebe. 'Daddy's on the radio!' I'd tell her and then she contentedly coo as Vernon began chatting and I prayed that he'd keep going a little longer and not put a record on just yet.

Once out and about I would always have a nice changing bag full of tricks: some food, a book, a toy and a drink. Anything that would buy me some time if I went for a coffee or was meeting someone and needed something to amuse or distract Phoebe for a bit.

Over time you become accustomed to what your little one will need and what will entertain them when you are out and about. You will also know your own (and your little one's) cut-off point when nothing else will do, you can no longer entertain them and they just want to scream and cry. I found with Phoebe – and I'm sure I'll soon be doing the same with Amber – that if I was out in a café or restaurant, an apologetic look to other customers would go a long way while I rummaged for my purse in order to pay and then I would get her in the pram or the car where she would fall asleep more often than not. It does seem that whenever babies or toddlers are beyond distraction it's for one of three reasons: their bum needs changing, they're hungry, or they're tired and no amount of reading *The Gruffalo* or singing 'Baa Baa Black Sheep' is going to help.

Little Personalities

Around this time Phoebe began to develop a definite personality of her own. It is strange to think that a baby, that can't speak or walk yet, can have a personality, but believe me she did. She was very spirited from an early age, she was constantly looking around for something to amuse her, and someone to do the amusing; she was never very good at amusing herself! We would go for lunch and no sooner had we put her in the high chair than she was demanding to get out again. Before you have children it's easy to think, when you're sitting in a restaurant and there is a child in there kicking up a fuss, that when you have kids you'll do it differently. You'll tell them to be quiet and then they'll sit there and behave themselves. But that is rarely the case once

Me, still in nappies age two!

He hasn't changed a bit!

they're here in all their glory. You sit in a restaurant, acutely aware of the other diners, hoping that your little darling will have the manners of someone who has just come out of finishing school. As Phoebe wasn't keen on being left in a high chair for more than a nanosecond I would quickly scoop her out and put her on my knee. Hence I ate most of my lunches accompanied by Phoebe for well over two years!

She has always been flamboyant and loves playing jokes on people. She has a very well-formed sense of humour for her age, and her and her dad love playing tricks on one another. She has a whoopee cushion that Vern bought her and a plastic ice cube with a fly in it that ends up in any newcomer's drink. She definitely gets her quirky sense of humour from her dad.

She is also very caring and will be the first person to give you a hug. She's always looking out for other people. She really looks out for other children at school too which is such a lovely trait to have and I'm really proud of her for that. Vernon says she's like me because she never stops for a minute, I might add he says this and as I turn to look at him I'm staring at the back of his retreating head; he can talk! Neither of us stop for a minute and Phoebe has definitely got that family trait.

Another example of her considerate nature was recently, when we were shopping for fish food at the local pet shop and she spotted a goldfish with only one eye. Nobody wanted this poor little fish, but Phoebe did. She felt sorry for it and promised to give it a good home, so we have *another* new addition to the family. The fish is known simply as One-Eyed Fish, following in the Binky tradition of not thinking too hard about pet names!

There are also a few things that she has said that are so specific to her and really make me smile, so I thought they were worth writing down. When we were discussing names for Amber, before she was born, Phoebe came into the kitchen and confidently announced that we didn't have to worry any longer, she had the perfect names for her new brother or sister. Curious to know that they might be Vern and I stopped and listened attentively. 'Cake Sunshine for a girl and Material for a boy,' she said matter-of-factly. Vernon and I thought this was hilarious and had to bite the inside of our cheeks to stop ourselves from laughing. Once, when I was pregnant with Amber, I was standing at the school gate with Phoebe and before I knew what she was doing she was pointing at my belly and announcing to all of the attendant kids and mums, 'Look at my mummy's fat belly everyone!' like a little town crier. I pulled my coat over my belly and smiled politely at everyone who was now staring at me.

The sweetest thing she said though was when Amber was born. She seemed to quite like the name Amber and so wasn't too disappointed that we hadn't called her Cake Sunshine. When she first saw her little sister she looked at me and said, 'She's as pretty as a thousand princesses'. I could have cried I thought this was such a sweet thing to say unprompted by me or Vernon. She really is her very own special little person.

In comparison to the rest of us Amber seems really calm and serene. I know that it is very early days, but she just has a way of looking at us that makes her seem not quite as hyper as the rest of her family. When she opens her eyes after a sleep she seems to take things in around her and seems to have a very calm, considered and content manner.

Vaccinations

Taking your baby for vaccinations for the first time can be traumatic, but it really is necessary to give them immunity to various, potentially life-threatening, infections. It is usually at eight weeks that they have their first vaccinations and at this time the only way they are really communicating with you is through those big trusting eyes. I remember taking Phoebe for her first injection very clearly. There she was, a little helpless bundle in my arms, and here I was big bad mummy taking her to be stabbed by the nasty nurse – or at least that's how I saw it. I sat her on my knee and the nurse chatted amiably to me while I was thinking: please just get it over with, my poor baby. She expertly jabbed the needle into Phoebe's leg and Phoebe gave me a momentary dazed look and then began to sob as if to say, how could you let her do that to me? I took her home feeling awful. Having spoken to other mums, everyone feels like this. You know that it is ultimately protecting your baby, but actually inflicting pain, however small, in order to protect them still sits uneasy as a mum. One way to comfort your baby while they have their vaccinations, that I've since heard about, is to breastfeed them.

We had all of Phoebe's injections, including MMR that is given at 13 months old. This is the combined jab for measles, mumps and rubella, which was once thought to have links to autism. The report that this claim came from has since been discredited, but the memory of these headlines are still something that mums naturally worry about. Vernon and I made an informed choice. I read up on the whole issue and took advice from our doctor. The unanimous medical view is that the combined jab was better than single jabs. Single jabs have to be administered a few weeks apart, during which time your little one can become susceptible to the illnesses they have yet to be inoculated for.

Amber had her first injection the other day. Vernon came with me and I think he was even more traumatized by the whole process than she was! She gave an ear-piercing scream and then cried her little heart out. Straight away afterwards she developed a fever and then had diarrhoea and was upset for the rest of the day. I felt terrible of course, but I know that it's just part and parcel of being a mum.

Sleep (Or Lack Thereof!)

When Phoebe was a newborn we expected to get – if not no sleep, then definitely broken sleep. If someone had told me that she would be three and a half before she slept through the night I would have probably cried and had myself admitted somewhere. I'd like to stress here that as far as I'm aware this isn't the norm, in fact I can't think of anyone else I've spoken to who had this problem. Most mums look at me with either abject horror or pity when I tell them of our sleepless years. And I think that we could definitely have done more when Phoebe was small to nip this in the bud, but by the time we realized what was happening, Phoebe was already set in a pattern of needing us to be with her to get to sleep and being distressed when she woke up and found that we weren't there.

When Phoebe was a tiny baby she would wake roughly every four hours for a feed. All babies have small tummies and need to feed regularly. But by the time they are between four and six months old they can take in more milk during the day and settle at night. There is no reason why a six-month-old baby cannot sleep for six or seven hours at a stretch, and some babies will even sleep from when you put them to bed right through to the morning by this age. The mistake I think that we made was that when we put her to bed we stayed with her until she fell asleep. It seemed like the right thing to do; we were by her side, comforting her. But when she awoke in the night and we weren't there she, unsurprisingly, became distressed until we reappeared.

As Phoebe became more aware of the world around her she became more aware of the fact that when she went to bed we would be there. We never really gave her the chance to settle herself, and by the time we realized this it seemed too late. She would cry relentlessly when we left the room. I read all the books and listened to all the advice, from Gina Ford to Dr Ferber's controlled crying methods (where you allow your child to cry for a short amount of time before going in to briefly comfort them and returning them to their cot), but nothing seemed to work. She never did settle herself, she would scream inconsolably for as long as we left her and would sound as if she was hyperventilating. It was heartbreaking and frustrating and we didn't know what to do.

Months went by and we were still going through the same nightly routine of having to be with Phoebe in order for her to fall asleep, then when she woke in the night we would go in and comfort her. We had created a pattern that we couldn't break. Every so often we would try the controlled crying method again and would be met with inconsolable tears. Rather than try to break the spirit of our amazingly willful daughter we just began to work around her; no doubt making things worse in the long run! The trouble is, when you are walking around in a zombie-like state it is hard to think of the bigger picture. I didn't want to think about what would happen if we left her to cry each night, until eventually she gave up and began to go to sleep on her own. For one thing I hated seeing her so distressed and also I just wanted us all to have the best night sleep we could on the night that faced us. I began to dread going to sleep knowing that I was half listening out for when Phoebe would wake up again and one of us would spring out of bed.

In between all of this we were both back at work, holding down jobs that meant appearing on TV and giving the impression that we were as fresh as daisies, while at home we were spending our lives in a sleep-deprived haze!

When Phoebe was about one and a half we decided to try and address this once and for all. We were going to try with all our might to get Phoebe to sleep. We made a pact: no matter how many times she cried we would persevere with the controlled crying method. We would pick her up, briefly console her and put her back in the bed and we would do this repeatedly until it became a habit for her. I don't know how many times you are meant to do this until your child gives in and goes to sleep, but we did it 45 times with no sign of Phoebe buckling. I couldn't do it for a 46th, she'd broken me and I brought her into bed with me. I was so disappointed. I felt like I must be letting her down in some way that there must be some trick that I was missing. But of course I know that that wasn't the case. We'd just left it too long, by which time Phoebe was so set in her ways that it was going to take an iron will – something that a very tired Vernon and I didn't have at the time – to break her pattern.

I know this may sound as thought I was giving in, but I promise you that wasn't the case; I didn't feel I had a choice. Sometimes I think that I'm crazy, that I should have paid for a night nurse to come and help us, but I just couldn't justify it to myself. We were Phoebe's parents and when she wasn't sleeping she didn't want some stranger, she wanted either myself or Vern. On the plus side, when she did come into our bed we did end up with loads of cuddles.

A few dazed months later Vernon and I were at a TV award show. Jo Frost, AKA Super Nanny, was there and we were like a

pair of stalkers trying to get to her. We couldn't sit still during the actual award ceremony, both fidgeting around trying to see where she was sitting. When we finally saw her we threw ourselves on her mercy. This poor woman must get parents at the end of their tethers pleading with her all the time, but I think we were particularly desperate. I begged her to tell me the secret to how to get Phoebe to sleep and she said that we had to be firm and keep putting her back in bed. Damn, her advice was consistent with everything I'd read. I wanted to invite her to our house, but I didn't want to be on some celebrity *Super Nanny* Christmas special where the world got to see Vernon and I padding up and down the corridor in the middle of the night!

As Phoebe got older we hoped that we would be able to explain to her why she needed to go to sleep. That in giving Mummy and Daddy a good night's sleep we'd be more fun the next morning, but I now realize that trying to explain and reason with a two and a half year old doesn't always work. She didn't understand what I was talking about, of course. To her she just wanted her mum and dad and the fact that she was now learning to speak meant that she could tell us how much she wanted us and where we were going wrong. We could be downstairs at ten o'clock at night and be settling down at the end of a long day and we'd hear Phoebe over the intercom saying, 'I've got real tears, Mummy!' I knew that other parents suffered in the same way. My sister once shut the door on her little boy, Finn, safe in the knowledge that the door handle was too high for him to reach. She found him later, out of his cot and asleep with his fingers just underneath the door ,as if the poor thing had been clawing his way out! Every other parent I spoke to assured me that they too had problem nights where their little ones didn't sleep but they

My nephews, Finn and Olly

eventually settled and slept through at some stage. But with Phoebe it didn't seem that that time was ever going to come.

She managed to negotiate her own escape route at an early age, using the nappy bin to stand on as she negotiated her way out of the cot. We didn't like shutting the door on her, not after my sister told me her story, so we bought a child gate in desperation! It was so that we could hear her in her room and she didn't feel locked in, but she also couldn't escape in the middle of the night and run into our bedroom! But she soon began to hang over the side of the safety gate, her face swollen with tears crying 'How can you leave me like this, I have real tears on my face?' I would lie there in bed for a moment, but then have to agree with her. How could I? And I'm actually laughing now while writing this! Looking back it was tough at the time, but it passes so quickly and eventually Vern and I got bored of talking about being tired and *actually* being tired. We didn't even discuss it in the end, it just became part of our life. We just worked and tried to sleep when we could and I'm sure our friends would say that we slipped off the social radar. In fact, I'd just like to take this opportunity to say sorry for being fairly absent friends, but honestly, we wouldn't have been much company!

There was often a new stage in her development that meant that her sleep might be justifiably broken. Teething, illness, starting nursery, wet bum when potty training. But that didn't stop it being frustrating that everyone else's child, who was the same age as Phoebe, seemed to be sleeping, while we were up with the milkman.

Writing about this now I can't believe we managed like this for three and a half years. But somehow we did. Vernon would let me go back to sleep for an hour in the morning, when he wasn't working, and I'd do the same for him. But I found it so difficult to accept outside help that I think I made things harder for myself than if I'd hired someone to help or let my mum come down and help me as she often offered to do. I suppose I was being strong willed, I wanted to care for Phoebe not anyone else, so maybe that's where she gets it from!

If you are reading this and it is filling you with dread please try not to worry too much! I really hope I'm not jinxing myself, but I'm confident it will be different this time. Already Amber is sleeping well – I know newborn babies do sleep a lot, but her whole demeanour is calm. I also think that Vern and I are calmer. We don't rush over to Amber thinking that she is choking just because she wants her dummy putting back in. We also put her to sleep in our bedroom, rather than allowing her to fall asleep with us downstairs and then putting her to bed. Even at this early stage she seems to know that this is where she goes to bed and that a darkened room signals time to go to sleep. The other thing that we are doing is leaving the room while Amber is still half awake. That way she won't expect us to be with her when she falls asleep, and therefore become distressed if she wakes up and we're not with her.

The other thing we have done this time around is chosen to take it in turns to sleep in our bedroom with Amber in the Moses basket while the other sleeps in the spare room and gets a full night sleep. This might not sound like the most romantic arrangement in the world, but in the first few months of a baby's life practicalities often come way above romance! It means that even if I have a really rough night with Amber I can at least look forward to a solid night's sleep the following day. I do think that sometimes the anticipation of not sleeping is worse than not sleeping itself. It is like self-inflicted torture, and having this arrangement means that we take away that panic. Obviously we have to be flexible, if one of us is working while the other is off then the one who isn't working is on baby duty, but on the whole we manage to split the work load fairly equably between us.

This time around I feel that everything is far more doable. Maybe it's because being a mum is now such second nature that I have established a routine for the girls without me realizing it, or maybe I'm just a lot more confident, but I find that I can manage my time and I have a lot more energy than I think I had the first time around.

Weaning and Introducing Solid Food

There are a number of different schools of thought on weaning; at the moment baby-led weaning is very popular. This means that the baby isn't introduced food in puréed form, but goes straight to whole bits of fruit and vegetables at around the age of six months. It may well work, but I didn't feel particularly comfortable with the idea of watching Phoebe trying to chomp on a piece of cucumber when all she'd had until then was breastmilk. So I decided to take the more traditional route and wean her using baby rice and purées.

It was when we were away in America with Vernon's work that I decided to start weaning Phoebe. She was five months old and she still loved her milk feeds, but she was getting increasingly hungry. You're supposed to start weaning when your baby is six months old, as they need the nutrients, but can do it from four months. I managed to track down some baby rice in a chemist and prepared it for her. It is actually nothing like rice, more like a fine powder than makes up like a thin porridge. I gave her a tiny spoonful and she instinctively knew to take it. She looked a little surprised at first, but then really took to it.

After a while I realized that I was going to have to branch out from just baby rice, as it is a little on the bland side. I would bake sweet potatoes and scoop out the insides. She would wolf this down and baked potatoes have always been a big hit with

Phoebe too. I would boil up different types of vegetables, purée them and feed them to her there and then. I always wanted to be organized and venture into a bit of batch cooking, but I never got round to it. I bought the ice-cube trays as I read this was a good way of freezing manageable portions, but it always seemed as easy to just cook what she needed when she needed it. I also bought a weaning tray with all the best intentions, but only used it twice.

However, this time with Amber I plan on being more adventurous. I have one of the Annabel Karmel cook books that offers advice on how to give weaning more variety and how to save yourself time. You can also find tips and recipes on her website annabelkarmel.com. When it came to introducing meat to Phoebe's diet I was initially a little torn. Having not eaten red meat myself for 20 years – and feeling quite smug about having avoided the chance of catching Mad Cow Disease – I wasn't sure if I was doing the right thing by feeding it to her, but I didn't want to make a choice for her at such a young age; I cook red meat for Vernon so don't have an actual problem with cooking it. I would buy the finest ground meat I could find and add it to her meals. The only thing I couldn't do was bring myself to taste it. I would poach fish in milk for her and add it to potato or carrots and broccoli. I knew it was important for her to have a variety of foods for all the different vitamins and nutrients.

When Phoebe was a baby I went in search of ready-made organic baby food and was shocked to find out that, at the time, there wasn't such a thing. I looked on the Internet and in specialist shops and really struggled to find anything. There was nothing I could just buy to throw in my bag when we were heading out. I was so shocked at the lack of availability I even looked into producing my own line of organic food, but the start-up costs were very expensive and by the time Phoebe was getting onto solid food there were already companies out there beginning to introduce organic baby food. Now there is every imaginable option for busy mums wanting a ready-made organic option for their little ones.

Plum baby food comes highly recommended from other mums. They have small pots that are great for when you're on the move. The small fruit pots are good to mix in with baby rice for breakfast when they are young. They also stock an organic baby porridge and muesli, which can help to add variety to your little one's diet. Ella's Kitchen do a variety of puréed food that comes in little pouches that can at first be squeezed out and spoon fed. Once your baby becomes more able to hold things they can also suck them like a drink. Marks & Spencer do really tasty organic ready meals for older babies and Hipp organic provide a range of food and snacks from finely puréed food to full meals for toddlers. Organix have a range of foods but their rice cakes and corn sticks are great for snacks on the go, but nothing beats bringing fruit out with you. A banana in your bag is always a good insurance policy – as is a ripe avocado and a spoon, an instant snack you can use as soon as you start weaning your baby.

As Phoebe got older Vern would joke that I never left the house without a ham sandwich. I would check that I had one, along with my purse and my keys. I found it quick to make and then, if I found myself stuck in traffic and Phoebe was getting a little peckish, I always had my trusty sandwich to hand. I tried to make sure that I used wholemeal or wholegrain bread though. Vernon is a big fan of white bread, good old Bolton's Warburton's in particular, but I always tried to make sure that anything I fed Phoebe wasn't just giving her empty calories that would see her hungry again an hour later.

I tried to give Phoebe water as an accompaniment to her meals, despite a dizzying array of juices available. However, when I did finally buckle and give her some apple juice watching her face was a joy; it was as if her taste buds had just come to life. She was reluctant to return to water once I'd provided her with this elixir, so I had to ration apple juice or at least heavily dilute it from then on – if she had the amount she wanted her teeth would have fallen out.

As Phoebe got older her appetite waned and she became more fussy in her eating habits. We had to employ more and more elaborate distraction techniques. 'Look Phoebe the airplane is coming ...', 'Look Phoebe here's the train ...', 'Brum, brum here comes the car ...' I think we went through every vehicle imaginable to get food into her. She was about two and a half when we started feeding her what we ate. There is no reason why you can't give your baby what you eat, just without added salt, but I tended to feed her earlier on, at about 5 p.m. and then Vernon and I would eat later when she was in bed. Now that she is older she isn't quite so fussy in her eating habits, but she's still not exactly experimental. If I ever give her some pizza with a rogue bit of basil on it then it will be picked off with a look of disdain. One meal she does love is fish and chips; she takes after her mum. And she calls mushy peas 'squashy peas' – I think this is so lovely that I can't bring myself to correct her. She'll be going off to college and asking for squashy peas if I have my way!

I think I've been quite diligent in what I've fed Phoebe, I try to cook organic food where possible and always used fresh ingredients where I can. I also subscribe to Abel & Cole, a weekly organic fruit and veg delivery service. When I think back to what I was brought up on, tinned or boiled-to-within-an-inch-of-their-lives vegetables I think that I might be being overcautious sometimes – it's not as if I ever came down with rickets. But I think if this sort of fresh food is available to me, then I owe it to the girls to cook for them as often as possible.

One example of a dish that I love to cook for Phoebe is slow baked chicken and vegetable casserole with a baked cheesy sweet potato. It's so easy. Just dice three or four chicken breasts and throw them it into an oven proof dish with some chicken stock, a tin of tomatoes, a clove of garlic and whatever vegetables you'd like in with it (I use carrots, leaks, broccoli and onion or whatever winter-type vegetables I happen to have in the fridge) and I allow it to slow cook for about two hours. I then bake the sweet potatoes for roughly an hour, depending on the size, scoop the insides out, mash it with cheddar cheese, put the mixture back in the jackets and finish them off under the grill. It's a really easy dish that doesn't take much faffing and is really tasty!

Parenting

Vernon and I didn't have any fixed ideas about parenting, but that's not to say that we were going to be woolly when it came to setting boundaries for our children. It was just that we both had such similar upbringings – clearly defined rules, in a loving environment without any sense of military strictness – that we felt we had a good sense of what would hopefully work now that we were parents. I have to admit that I'm softer than Vernon and discipline doesn't come naturally to me. I think this stems from my mum telling me as a kid that if I was naughty I would go to the 'naughty girls' home'. She'd even talk about this place as if it was some far away fictitious house that I might encounter one day if I was really naughty; she actually used to point to a building on the way into town and tell me that this was where all the naughty girls were housed. I lived in fear of the place. Once, when my mum had bought me the worst outfit in the world – purple crimpleen trousers that I refused to wear and then proceeded to cover in biro just to make sure they were unwearable – she actually put in a fake call to the naughty girls' home. She was probably calling the speaking clock, but I totally believed her; I was terrified. It was only years later that I found out that the 'naughty girls' home' was actually an old people's home. Either that or those poor girls had been there a long, long time.

So Vern is the disciplinarian with Phoebe, not that he's standing over her with a stick getting her to tidy her room, but she knows that when he says something, he means it and she shouldn't try to push him. That said, she also has the most fun with her dad and laughs so much when she's with him that she doesn't see him as anything like an authoritarian figure, just the most likely out of the two of us to tell her off.

We often play good cop bad cop (I'm not sure if this is something that comes highly recommended by child psychologists when it comes to parenting, but it works for us!) Me in the role of good cop on Phoebe's side saying things like, 'Well I don't think she meant it when she did that …' And Vernon taking a more serious stance saying 'Well she knows she's not allowed to do that'. While we both throw each other knowing looks over her head. The thing with Phoebe is that she is generally a good girl and doesn't need much in the way of chastisement. I just like to keep her in check, and will do the same with Amber. One of the most important things to me and Vernon when it comes to parenting and discipline is that we instil politeness and courtesy in our girls. I'd hate to have a child who thought that she could say what she wanted to others and not mind her Ps and Qs.

One thing that did work for us from when Phoebe was about two was a wall chart with gold stars on it that meant she could earn points if she ate all her dinner, slept in her own bed, helped me put her books back on the shelf. Little goals, but ones that helped instil a sense of order and cooperation. We found this really useful as she got a real sense of achievement and feeling grown up by doing things that meant she would be rewarded. It was also a very positive way of teaching her to do things without telling her off for not doing certain things.

This is something that is easy to implement once a child is around two years old. Before that it is hard to explain in a way that they can fully understand, and I always think telling off small children should be a last resort. Obviously, if they are hitting you in the face in the middle of Tesco and screaming blue murder you are not inclined to want to say 'There, there, darling' and let them carry on. But they are so small and have such limited ways in which to display their emotions that sometimes they come out in ways that could test a saint. I tried to be clear from an early age with Phoebe when she was doing something that I thought was wrong, but I think it is only when she could communicate verbally that we could successfully show her right from wrong.

Being able to communicate verbally, however, brings with it its own problems. Vern and I tried the naughty step and found that Phoebe would sit on it and cry, employing her 'I have real tears on my face' speech that was always guaranteed to make me crumble. Friends who have boys think this is such a hilariously female thing to do at such an early age. In my very unscientific straw poll, boys, on the whole, serve their time on the naughty step counting down the seconds until they can get off again. While girls resort to emotional blackmail!

Phoebe is such a kind and good little girl though, and looks for the good in everything, so I find it hard to get angry with her and just like to make sure that she is being well behaved. All children push boundaries to see how far they can get with their mum and dad, but I think, so far, we've done quite well in making sure Phoebe is happy, well rounded and has fun without ever resorting to being cheeky. I'd hate to think that my girls were bound by military rules and were scared to have an opinion because they were used to being told off. I think that we've managed to get the balance right with Phoebe and hopefully we'll do the same with Amber.

Reading and Playing

All of my best memories from childhood involve playing in some way, shape or form. Whether it was messing around in the garden with my sister and dad, or packing up a flask and sandwiches and heading out for the day somewhere exotic and far afield like Chester Zoo. So now I'm a mum I'm an absolute sucker for a day out. I'm forever packing Phoebe up and taking her somewhere. In fact only the other day I had Amber, all of two months old, and Phoebe at London Zoo. Phoebe of course is now an aficionado of animals of all shapes and sizes, whereas poor Amber is still focusing on things and wondering what on earth I'm talking about as I point all of the different sights out to her. I think she was similarly impressed when, at three weeks old, I had her at the park throwing bread for the ducks. It seems so natural to me to do this from an early age with the girls.

Vernon is a great laugh to be around and his sense of fun and joy is infectious. It is particularly great to see him with Phoebe playing rough and tumble and making her laugh uncontrollably. He could play from the moment he wakes up to the moment he goes to bed. I think that fun and play are so important for children; it's how they learn. While Vernon is more at home playing aeroplanes and whoopee cushions with Phoebe, I'll get stuck in with paints and pens and making costumes. Phoebe loves to dress up and make things; and I've realized that a little girl just simply can't have enough glitter pens. I'm also quite partial to having a go on the trampoline. Have you seen children's trampolines now? I would have killed for one of those as a kid. They're great and not like the bouncy death traps they

Vernon age five, look at those legs!

Vernon playing, age seven

used to have at sports centres when I was younger. They come with a protective net, which means your little ones can't get over enthusiastic and end upside down on the ground after two bounces. There's something about playing and being silly with your own children that taps into how you felt as a child yourself, and I love it.

Our holidays are now all about play and fun. Of course we try to get a little bit of time to ourselves for a meal together, but holidays now are definitely about the children. We even took Phoebe on holiday to the Isle of Wight – where I'd holidayed for so many years with my family – to take her to the places that I remember loving as a girl. It was great to see the place again through a child's eyes, to take her to the little café where I remember sitting as a girl and watch how much pleasure she got from simple things like eating ice cream, spotting sea gulls or watching the sea crash on the sand. Seeing how Phoebe reacted to this magical place from my childhood made me realize how great the holidays must have been for my mum and dad every year, and what enjoyment they must have got from these trips. More than that though it made me realize what Mum and Dad did for me and my sister. Becoming a parent myself has really made me appreciate everything my parents did for me. When you're little you just think that your mum and dad are your mum and dad and that's that. It's only when you're in that position yourself that you realize how much they put into being with us and for my parents play, fun and holidays were a big part of that.

I love reading with Phoebe and introduced her to books at an early age; I am already doing the same with Amber. I would have her propped up looking at the pictures in the book while I read out the stories, not sure whether she had a clue or not about what was going on. But as she got older and became more aware of things, she quickly chose her own favourites that she would grab from the bookshelf and waddle over to me, holding them out to be read. Now I love nothing more than sitting in the children's section of Waterstone's choosing books with Phoebe. She really likes *Guess How Much I Love You?*, which is a really sweet book about a mummy and baby rabbit telling each other how much they love one another. She is also rather partial to a book that I found called *Rastamouse* by Michael De Souza, which is hilarious. When I was younger I loved Enid Blyton's *The Wishing Chair* and *The Folk of the Far Away Tree* and Phoebe is now at an age when I can read these classics to her. I think that they are such magical stories.

Phoebe also loves anything with a princess in so *The Little Mermaid* and anything Disney based is usually a hit. In fact, returning to the idea of our holidays geared around the children, Vernon and I took Phoebe to meet the princesses at Disney World. I know that it's Disney and it's a big money-making enterprise, but honestly, when you're there and you see your little girl so utterly transported by this world it is really wonderful. Seeing all of these little girls queuing to see the princesses was like watching them wait to see their favourite band live in concert. They were all so excited. And that excitement rubbed off on me and Vern so much that by the time the different Disney Princesses – Ariel from *The Little Mermaid*, Snow White, Jasmine from *Aladdin*, Cinderella, and more – came out to sit with the girls and eat lunch the atmosphere was at fever pitch and Vernon and I had tears in our eyes!

Someone else that Phoebe loved when she was a little younger was Barney. Barney is a big purple dinosaur who teaches children about loving and being kind to one another. We managed to secure some tickets to see Barney at Tower Hill music festival. We trekked into London, clutching the tickets with a very excited Phoebe, but this outing wasn't to be nearly as successful as our lunch with the princesses. Barney, like a fading rock god who's lost touch with his audience, only came on for two songs and then wandered off again. Me and Vern even grumbled to one another that we weren't sure it was the real Barney. But we tried to brush over our own disappointment at the big purple let down and assured Phoebe that Barney must have been tired because he'd come all the way from America on a plane and that was why he'd only managed to do one limp little dance for his adoring fans. Not to be defeated we did eventually track down the real Barney, in Florida at Universal Studios, and he certainly didn't disappoint!

I'm looking forward to having all these play firsts all over again with Amber. At the moment she is just beginning to focus and lies calmly on her play gym batting her toys. She hates being put in a chair and screams, her eyes out on stalks if we try to secure her in one. She likes being laid down by the picture window that looks out on our garden to look at the trees. She seems mesmerized by the movement of the trees and the shadows. I show her picture books and she looks wide-eyed at them, so hopefully she is getting something from them. She loves lots of one to one play and attention and being sung to. I sing little lullabies to her all the time. I know that she is very young and doesn't understand, but is piecing the world together day by day. I think that play is an integral part of that process from an early age and hopefully she will have the same sense of fun and play that Phoebe has.

Toys

We didn't go too toy crazy the second time around. Vernon did buy a Winnie the Pooh baby gym, which Amber lies on frantically kicking the toys, but we already had loads of toys from when Phoebe was small that Amber could play with. With Phoebe we started off with a few basics, accumulated stuff as presents and bought other bits and bobs along the way. There is always the temptation to try to be stylish and minimalist when it comes to toys, thinking that your little one will only ever play with a wooden train from the White Company or a designer toy from Habitat. But once your baby is up and running, and heading for the toy box, if he or she is anything like mine they will hone in on the most plastic, garish thing they can find. Babies don't care too much about your desire to have a nice *Hello!* spread house. So ditch the neutral tones as babies are stimulated by colours and contrasting patterns. It won't be there for ever, and at least you can pack it all away in a toy box at the end of the day.

You may find you receive some interesting presents for your little one that you wouldn't have necessarily chosen yourself. The funniest gift we received for Phoebe was a 1m (3ft), stone garden gnome. Vernon's mum turned up at the door one day with said gnome in tow. It was so heavy that it took three grown men to carry it into the garden and place it under the tree where it still sits today, looking like a strange shrunken human. Vernon's mum said, 'I bought him for Phoebe, but I think he has a look of cousin Billy.' So the gnome was christened Billy. He freaked me out a bit at first, and I couldn't even look him in the eye when I went out in the garden. But Phoebe grew to love him and we have pictures of her when she is really young pointing at him in wonder. Billy might not be something that I would have picked out in a line up as ideal six-month-old-baby toy material but he is now part of the family and we wouldn't be without him watching over the garden.

Style for Little Ones

There are so many beautiful affordable children's clothes out there these days that it is easy to dress your children well, even on a budget. Everywhere from Primark and H&M, through to fashion labels like Gucci and D&G, have children's clothes ranges. I loved dressing Phoebe up in gorgeous dresses with sequins and sparkles when she was small and I'm doing the same now with Amber, but I'd never want my girls to look like an extension of some designer wardrobe I was trying to work myself. It doesn't sit easy with me when I see children dressed like little peacocks, knowing that their mums have forced them into it. That said, most little girls, given half a chance, would chose something more befitting a Mardi Gras parade than something they should be wearing to play out in if they had free reign to choose their own clothes. Trying to explain to a three-year-old why a sequinned all-in-one and angel wings isn't something she can wear to nursery isn't always the easiest task.

I find shopping for little girls' clothes endlessly exciting. Nearly every shop you go in these days has gorgeous girly clothes. And sequinned shoes are ten-a-penny. I remember when I was a little girl coveting a pair of silver sparkly shoes that I saw in a specialist dance shop when we were in town shopping. I would marvel at these shoes, my nose pressed to the window, wondering what one had to do to own such a thing. Phoebe has an array of sparkly shoes and I have to admit, even as her mother, to a tinge of jealousy. I wouldn't be above trying them on if I thought they'd fit. In fact Phoebe has had so much pink, sparkle and glitter in her wardrobe from an early age that I'm sure she'll rebel and become a Goth by the time she's 14, refusing to wear anything other than black!

Phoebe has had a strong opinion on what she wanted to wear from an early age. Even when she was two she was adamant that she wouldn't wear some skinny leg jeans that I'd bought her and thought would look really cool on her. I've already decided that I'm going to avoid dressing-up dramas with Amber as much as possible. Instead of giving her a choice of a couple of outfits as I would with Phoebe I'm just going to decide for her. Phoebe loves clothes and dressing up and has her own take on what she likes. She will even customize her own clothes – not that she knows that's what she's doing or that I won't allow out of the door in her 'creations'. She'll parade into the lounge with a scarf draped around her and a belt around her waist and ask 'Mummy, is this fashion?' before doing a little twirl and exiting again to see what else she can find to make a new ensemble out of.

When shopping for babies and toddlers I definitely think it is best to stick to high-street stores. They grow so quickly that no matter how beautiful a designer cardigan might be it is hard to justify its purchase in relation to how long it will be worn for. Zara and H&M both do great kids' ranges that are affordable and look great. The White Company are great for little girl nighties, and for boys pyjamas too. You may pay a premium, but I always find that their clothes wash and wash and really last. Baby Gap is great for pretty much everything you could need from newborn upwards and a great tip is that their socks stay on. Most baby socks shoot off within minutes, but whatever Gap have done, they've managed to design a sock that stays put. Marks & Spencer do great children's clothes that are funky,

Karen, two-and-a-half, and me age five

Looking very co-ordinated on holiday!

affordable and again wash really well.

Asda do a good range of children's clothes and also seem to be the best place to get *High School Musical* stuff – anyone with a girl over the age of three will tell you this sort of knowledge is invaluable.

Having said that I was loathed to go down a designer route, I have to hold my hands up and confess to buying Phoebe a few designer pieces here and there, but it was usually in the sale! With regard to designer gear: if you're adamant that you want something a bit more upmarket, then TK MAXX do designer baby wear. Obviously there is no guarantee which labels you will get, but they are always well discounted and a mum that I know, who has boys, says it is the only place she shops for jeans. They also sell discounted Grobags and, other than various websites, I can't think of anywhere else I've seen them discounted.

It is hard when clothing little girls not to succumb to pester power and let them dress like mini Pussycat Dolls. Especially when even magazines for very young children give away free lip gloss and face glitter. But neither would I want poor Phoebe walking around dressed like something from *Little House on the Prairie*. So I try to strike a balance, to let her know the difference between dress up and real clothes and to let her have her glitter and sequins, but be mindful to dress her comfortably and age appropriately. There's lots of time to grow up and just because she might have the cast of *High School Musical* on her T-shirt doesn't mean she gets to dress like one of them.

Karen and I on a walk in the Peak District

Baby
Number
Two

Deciding to Have Another Baby

Although we had countless broken nights of sleep with Phoebe the decision to have another baby wasn't something we struggled with. After all, it would be wonderful to add to our little family and we knew Phoebe would welcome the company and make a great, big sister.

We didn't make a concerted plan to have baby number two. There were no charts or ovulation kits or any of that sort of thing. In fact, at first I was very laid back about the whole thing; if it happened then it happened. In a weird way I didn't want to push my luck in wanting another baby and felt grateful that we already had such a happy and healthy girl. Then we began to come around to the idea of *really* having another baby and how it would feel for us to be four instead of three. Both Vernon and I had siblings, and most of our fond childhood memories were wrapped up in things that had happened with them. So we decided to try again. We tried to shut out the idea that we would ever have to go back to having broken sleep for three and a half years again, and decided to take the plunge.

I had to take Dostinex again because my prolactin levels had not righted themselves without intervention, and then we set about baby making. I didn't think I'd get pregnant again as quickly as I had the first time. I've no idea what I was basing that on, I just didn't! I think I just thought that, with erratic hormone levels, I might just have been lucky with Phoebe. But again I got pregnant within a few months of returning to taking the miracle tablet.

When I found out that I was pregnant I was ecstatic and the whole pregnancy, despite suffering from Boomerang flu, was a far more laid back experience than the first time around and it seemed to go more quickly .

In the two short months since Amber arrived there have been a few incidents that have proved to me that, just because we had Phoebe, there are still lots of things to learn with every new baby.

So Far with Amber...

'Poogate'

'Poogate' is what Vernon and I now jokingly call the time when Amber was very little and she simply didn't poo for two weeks. We can joke about it now, but at the time it was very worrying. Brand-new babies expel something called meconium in their first couple of nappies. It's more of a thick, tarry substance than normal poo, but for the purpose of learning to nappy change it might as well be. Amber had a couple of these and then after that she just had wet nappies. At first I didn't think much of it, I was struggling to breastfeed and thought that she might not be getting enough milk in order to form a proper poo. But after more than a week of this I began to worry. I took her to the doctor and he sent me to the hospital, which was nerve-racking to say the least! There, the doctor gave her a suppository. She was so tiny, it didn't seem right having something inserted inside her in this way, the poor little mite. Still, it had the desired effect almost immediately.

The doctor suggested that her digestive system might be blocked, which was alarming, and if there wasn't an improvement in a week I should come back. A week! That was an age for a baby that was only a couple of weeks old. Also, I didn't want to get into a cycle of giving Amber suppositories, it felt too violent, she was too small. And anyway, I wanted it to happen naturally so that her body was doing it rather than being forced by intervention. I felt guilty, that I wasn't giving her enough milk and this was somehow contributing to her distress. I decided to seek a second opinion.

The second doctor was far more reassuring. He told me something which no one had mentioned: breastfed babies can take longer to poo. Not only that, but babies can poo anything from eight times a day to about once a fortnight, which is entirely normal. Once I was armed with this information I began to talk to other mums about it, many told me that they had had this problem. Some said it took months for their babies to become regular. The doctor asked me to describe what else was happening and I told him about Amber's discomfort and the little distressed noises she was making as if she was trying to poo, but it just wasn't working. He said that it sounded to him like her digestive system wasn't blocked at all, but that she might be suffering from something called gastric reflux. He suggested that we let her sleep at a slight angle, so her head, in the Moses basket, was higher than her feet. This would mean that any acids that were giving her trouble wouldn't rise and upset her further.

We took her home and hoped that this would help ease her discomfort. I massaged her tummy in a clockwise direction and moved her legs around in a circular motion, both of which I'd read somewhere might help. I was receiving texts from both grandmas anxious to know if there'd been any poo developments. I had Vern's aunt suggesting we give her rosehip water and the doctor telling me she'd have gum disease if we did that. I had a midwife saying that, although it wasn't something that was recommended nowadays, years ago cooled boiled water with a bit of brown sugar was advised for babies that weren't pooing (now they use a drop of orange juice). Nothing seemed to work. I was beginning to worry that she might have a serious problem that no one seemed to know how to deal with. Amber was two

weeks old when she finally filled her nappy and the relief
was unbelievable. I was so proud of her – I'm sure she'll
be really pleased to know that when she's older. I'd been so
worried about her and thought that we might have to resort
to suppositories or, worse, she might be taken into hospital.
But she managed it all on her own and since then, touch
wood, she has been nice and regular.

Meningitis Scare

This happened only a few days ago. Vernon was away in Ibiza
working with Radio 1 for the weekend and I was to have Amber
and Phoebe on my own for the first time since Amber was born.
I was quite looking forward to it and so was Phoebe. She loves
helping out with Amber and I was planning a weekend in with
the girls. Vernon went away on Friday and was returning on
Sunday night. On Saturday I started to notice that Amber wasn't
well. She had cold hands and feet, she wasn't taking any milk,
she was really sleepy and she had diarrhoea, which after
Poogate was a first. She also had a raised red rash. I looked all
of these symptoms up and realized that it all pointed towards
meningitis. I tried not to panic, but I was terrified. I did the glass
test (you roll a glass over the rash and if it is a meningitis or
septicaemia rash it won't blanch in colour – other forms of rash
lose their colour) and to my horror the colour stayed the same.
I quickly got Amber and Phoebe's stuff together, plonked them
in the car and set off to the hospital. I was so panicked that I put
the alarm on with the dog still in the house and had to deal with
a phone call from the police en route. I was trying to remain as
composed as I possibly could so that I didn't panic Phoebe, but

it was hard. I got to the hospital as quickly as I could, threw the car into the car park and bundled the girls into A&E, resisting the urge to shoulder barge everyone else out of the way; I just wanted someone to tell me that my baby was going to be all right. Vernon had been calling me to check in and see how we were all doing, but I'd been unable to take the call because I knew that I would only worry him so I decided to call him once I'd spoken to a doctor.

We were seen by a triage nurse and then only had to wait 20 minutes to see a doctors, newborn babies are obviously given priority in A&E.

I was convinced that they were going to tell me she had meningitis so I was trying my best not to panic and to stay focused so I could listen to the advice I would be given. They did some tests to monitor Amber's blood; when the tests came back I was told that, despite the glass test, she didn't have meningitis. They said they'd like to keep her in for a little while more just for observation and asked me if I would feed her. She hadn't been feeding, but as soon as the nurse pulled the curtains around me she latched on, I was so relieved. After about an hour we were told that she had a viral infection and we were free to go. The doctor didn't offer much more than that other than I should keep my eye on her and it would clear up. I was just relieved we were being allowed to go home and that she wasn't suffering from something serious and potentially life threatening.

Poor Amber. She's only eight weeks old and she's already been back to hospital twice. I've only had to go to hospital with Phoebe once and that was when, at nine months old, she sliced her hand on a tin of baby food when my back was turned for a second. She had to have her finger bandaged and was given a tetanus shot, but she hasn't been back since. The thing that freaked me out that time was that I didn't even know where the hospital was. That's one bit of advice I would give, if you are moving to a new area, do a dummy run to the hospital because chances are at some stage you will end up in A&E, even if it's only because they've got a pan stuck on their head!

Having Two Children

Amber is such a gorgeous little thing and has such a little personality of her own that it's already hard to imagine life before she was around. A lot of mums said this to me before she came along, but it is true: two children doesn't mean double the work. We already had our own framework of family life that we had worked hard at for the past four and a half years with Pheobe, and Amber has slipped into this rather than create more massive life changes.

It is hard sometimes to look after both Phoebe and Amber together because they often need different things at different times, but Phoebe is very patient and understanding and this makes life easier. Of course it is an adjustment for Phoebe too, because for so long it has been just her and her mum and dad. But I have to say she is doing brilliantly and loving being a big sister. I just can't wait until she is older and she and Amber can be great friends and playmates like me and Karen were when growing up. But even as I'm writing this I'm mindful to not want to wish their lives away. It's lovely to see Phoebe now, being gentle with her sister and wanting to help me with her. And she is a really big help. So thanks Phoebe!

20/6/2009

Epilogue

So here I am at the end of the book. And it really has been a bit of a roller coaster revisiting all the things that happened throughout my pregnancies and early days as a mum. It has made me remember how precious those times were with Phoebe and are now with Amber. I know it's a cliché, but the time when your children are small really does fly by and I'm glad to say that, as sleep deprived as I was, I haven't forgotten any of those precious memories.

I am also happy to report that the sleeplessness and abyss staring that I was doing at the start of the book has become a far less frequent an occurrence and even though it's early days and Amber is still only three months old I feel as though we are doing well and her routine is such that she might even sleep through the night someday soon.

When we had Phoebe she added a new dimension to our relationship. We went from just having to think about ourselves to having another little person to think about and care for – we were a family and it felt good. But when it was just the three of us all of our attention was, obviously, lavished on Phoebe. Now that Amber is here it feels like she is the icing on our family cake. Phoebe has a sister, who she can play with, fight with, grow up with and love, and we have 'children'. The fact that we now talk in plural about children, rather than just Phoebe, sometimes makes me and Vernon giggle. Having 'children' is a serious business. That's the stuff of being a proper grown up.

There are a few things that I've definitely learned and can now implement second time around. I think the most important

thing is not to make a rod for your own back in whatever it is you are doing. And this doesn't just apply to when you are trying to establish a sleep routine, which is obviously the big thing that I would do differently. It's little things like not making your baby accustomed to only drinking warm milk. When Phoebe was little Vernon's mum gave her a bottle of warmed milk, bless her heart she was just doing her best for her beloved granddaughter, but after that my life became ruled by where we could find a microwave. I'm sure that one of Phoebe's first full sentences was 'Do you have a microwave please?' She just wouldn't take a cold bottle after that. I won't be making the same mistake with Amber, she'll be having cold milk as soon as I've stopped breastfeeding. My sister feeds her youngest cold baby food. When I turned my nose up at this she rightly pointed out that he doesn't know any different. And as it works for them and make's Karen's life easier then great. I'm also not quite as militantly bashful when it comes to breastfeeding, but that's something that came over time rather than something I decided to do.

I've also reached a few of my own personal goals in the past few weeks that make me feel that I'm edging back to being myself. The first one to report is that I managed to get back in my Top Shop Baxter skinny jeans (cue trumpet fanfare!) I have to come clean and admit that in order fasten them I had to lie on the bedroom floor with one foot up against the wardrobe and I walked like John Wayne for a good 15 minutes after getting them on, but they were on.

Another thing I did a few weeks ago was I played on a trampoline with Phoebe. So what? You might think. But I'd heard numerous horror stories from other mums about natural birth meaning that you'll never look at a trampoline the same way again. I'll just say, strong pull of gravity and lax undercarriage muscles don't go hand in hand. So it was with some trepidation that I climbed on Phoebe's trampoline and attempted my first bounce. Phoebe didn't think anything of it, she was used to Mummy joining her on the trampoline; I was terrified. But I jumped and I landed and then jumped again and landed again and I can happily report that everything was as it had always been. Phew!

Going to my first work meeting and putting on some high heels and taking with me my favourite bag (Marc Jacobs, patent, gorgeous) with my phone, some keys and a lip gloss in it, made me feel normal again. It was great to sit down with other adults, reach into my bag and not have to fight my way past scented nappy bags and baby wipes, or to pull out a pen only to see a breast pad land in the lap of a BBC executive. It did feel like a bit of a milestone being out in the world on my own, but I was on the phone as soon as I left home and although I was only away for a few hours I asked Vernon to send me some pictures of Amber – well I didn't want her doing something and me to have missed it!

It is so nice to begin to get out and about in the world again both with the girls and on my own but my first port of call now is home. I'm constantly wondering and worrying about the girls. I'm really enjoying our family life now and looking forward to the great times I know are ahead for us and for the girls as sisters.

I hope that some of this book has been of use to you, even if it was just so that you could immerse yourself in someone else's experience of birth and motherhood, which as I've said was always my favourite thing to do when I was pregnant. And if any of the tips on where to shop or get advice have been handy then I've provided a few websites in the back of the book for quick reference.

One thing I would say is that no matter how daunting it all seems at this moment in time, as you stare down at your bump and wonder how on earth you will manage when your baby is out in the world, is that you will more than manage. Becoming a mum will be scary, life-changing, shattering and uplifting, but it is ultimately the best thing you will ever do.

In the first few weeks it might feel like you're taking two steps forward and three back, but you will get there. And then one day you'll suddenly catch yourself and you will be in the car, baby in tow, baby bagged packed (with enough stuff for the day ahead rather than a two-week break) your hair washed and dried, make-up on and you will have barely thought how you achieved all of this; it will be just part of what you do. You will start to feel like your old self again, only now you will have a gorgeous baby who will be part of your life for ever and that is the most wonderful thing of all.

List of Useful Websites

Help and support
NHS Direct www.nhsdirect.nhs.uk
NCT (National Childbirth Trust)
   www.nctpregnancyandbabycare.com
Bliss (premature babies) www.bliss.org.uk.
Tamba (Twins and Multiple Births Association)
   www.tamba.org.uk
FSID (The Foundation for the Study of Infant Deaths)
   www.sids.org.uk
NHS Breastfeeding www.breastfeeding.nhs.uk
La Leche League www.lalecheleague.org.uk
Baby Centre www.babycentre.co.uk
Net Mums www.netmums.com

Maternity wear, treats and baby things
ASOS www.asos.com
Net-A-Porter www.net-a-porter.com
Formes www.formes.com
Isabella Oliver www.isabellaoliver.com/maternity-clothes
Lula Sapphire www.lulasapphire.com
Mamas and Papas www.mamasandpapas.com
Mama-la-mode www.mama-la-mode.com
Mothercare www.mothercare.com
Zara for Kids www.zara.com
The White Company www.thewhitecompany.com
The Great Little Trading Company www.gltc.co.uk
Oioi www.oioi.com.au

Holidays
Baby-friendly Boltholes www.babyfriendlyboltholes.co.uk
Baby Goes Too www.babygoes2.com

Baby food
Annabel Karmel www.annabelkarmel.com
HiPP Organic www.hipp.co.uk
Ella's Kitchen www.ellaskitchen.co.uk

Index

alcohol, pregnancy and 19, 37, 40, 41
anxiety, birth 13, 31–3, 79, 123
appetite during pregnancy 26, 33–5
ASOS 33, 65
♡
Back to Reality 19, 20
bags, baby 182–3
bathing your baby 158
BBC 42–3, 55, 196, 278
birth 128–51
    'advice', dealing with 78–81
    anxiety over 13, 79, 123
    classes, preparation 69
    due date 58
    epidural 13, 79, 118, 127, 130, 131,
        134, 142, 146, 147, 150
    final week 125–6
    going back on your plans 80–1
    hospital, preparing for 108–19
    labour pains 13
    natural 13, 76–7, 137–51
    pain relief 13, 79–80, 118, 127, 130,
        131, 134, 142, 146, 147, 150
    planning for 69–70, 80–1,
        108–19, 127
    waters breaking 80–1
Birth Stories 27, 28, 82, 118, 123
blues, baby 191–4
bottles and sterilizers 162, 174, 202
breastfeeding 162–73, 184, 191 see
    also feeding your baby
breasts, engorgement during
    pregnancy 14

bringing your baby home 154, 157–8
Bugaboo pram 92, 93
♡
Caesarean section 13, 70, 75, 79–80,
    102, 118, 123, 124, 125, 127,
    130–6, 137, 143, 146, 149, 157
childcare 187–8, 190, 196
Children in Need 28, 30
clothes:
    for little ones 96–7, 254–5, 258
    in the second trimester 65–7
    in the third trimester 98, 100
confidence in parenting 202–3
contraception 23
cot:
    death 185
    positioning in 14
    travel 93
cravings and aversions 33–4
crying, baby 226, 227, 228–33
♡
Daly Beauty range 122
Dickenson, David 71, 96
digestive system, child 264–6
discipline 241–3
Dostinex 25, 28, 262
Down's Syndrome 58
du Beke, Anton 27, 28, 30
due date 58
dummy, using a 184–5
♡
emotional impact of pregnancy
    and birth 26, 31–3, 79, 170, 172

epidural 13, 79, 118, 127, 130, 131,
     134, 142, 146, 147, 150
exercise 68
expressing milk 165–9
     ♡
feeding your baby 14, 202
     bottles and sterilizers 162,
          174, 202
     breastfeeding 162–73, 184, 191
     dummies and 184
     'expressing' 165–9
     first few weeks 162–9
     'nipple confusion' 174
     solids 202, 236–40
     travelling and 208–9
     weaning 236–40
feet, caring for during
     pregnancy 101
fertility 23
final week before birth 125–6
first trimester: weeks 1 to 13 18–59
Flower Fairies furniture 105
fontanelle 157
food 283
     to be avoided 34–5
     cravings and aversions 33–4
     grocery shopping during
          pregnancy 103–4
     vitamins 35–6
     see also feeding your baby
Forsyth, Bruce 27, 42, 43, 71, 197
Frost, Jo 228, 230
     ♡
gastric reflux 14
GMTV 27
GP (doctor) 18, 181–2

Grill, The 20, 32
Grobags 14, 177
     ♡
heartburn 14, 120–1
holidays with children 49, 202,
     204–9, 210–15, 248, 283
     feeding your child on 208–9
     flying with children 204–9
     occupying children while
          travelling 215, 218–19
home, preparing for baby 21, 157
hospital, preparing for 108–19
     baby bag (things you need)
          110–17, 142
     checking into 130
     father's role in 109–10
     getting to 13, 198
     hospital notes and birth
          plan 114, 118–19
     ♡
kick, feeling baby for the
     first time 82–3
     ♡
La Leche League 173
labour pains 13
lochia 113
     ♡
Maclaren buggy 93, 205–6
Make Me a Supermodel 167
Mamas & Papas 92, 96–7, 98, 183
Marks & Spencer 27, 48, 66, 97,
     122, 165, 238, 255
maternity wear 282–3
McCall, Davina 80
McPherson, Elle 67
meningitis 266–8

midwife 80, 115, 118, 145, 150, 163, 169
MMR jab 224–5
monitors, baby 94–5
mood swings 31–3, 170, 172
morning sickness 19, 26–31
Moses basket 92, 176, 177, 181, 185
mumsnet.com 31

♡

names, baby 15, 21, 73–4
nannies 187–8
napping 36–7
National Childcare Trust (NCT) 69
nesting 37
neural tube defects 58
NHS 58, 142
    direct 120
    preparation for birth classes 69
    scans 58
night nurse 187–8
nipple confusion 174
nursery, 105, 107, 190

♡

outside help 187–8, 190, 196

♡

panicking 13, 14, 31, 79, 123, 180–1
parenting/discipline 241–3
periods, pregnancy and 23, 24–5
personalities, little 220–3
Phone Zone 54–5
physical changes, pregnancy induced 22
playing with children 244–50
'Poogate' 264–6
post-natal depression 170, 190
prams and buggies:

assembling 180–1
choosing a 92–3
on holiday 205–6
Pregnacare tablets 36
pregnancy 18–47
    alcohol and 19, 37, 40, 41
    appetite during 26
    baby kick, feeling for the first time 82–3
    body, changes to during 14, 62–4
    contraception and 23
    cravings and aversions 33–4
    discovering your 18–31
    emotional impact of 26, 31–3, 170, 172
    irregular periods and 23, 24–5
    maladies 62–3
    mood swings 31–3, 170, 172
    morning sickness 26–31
    physical changes, outward 22
    preparing for 23–5
    prolactin and 24–5, 28, 262
    smell, sense of 26, 34
    socialising during 40–2
    tests 13, 18, 19
prolactin 24–5, 28, 262
prostaglandins 137, 145

♡

reading and playing with children 244–50
retail therapy 33

♡

scans:
    finding out sex of baby 84–6
    first 58–9
    second 84–6

second child 260–79
    deciding to have 262–3
    having two children 270
second trimester: weeks 14 to 27
        60–87
sex of baby, finding out 84–6
six months onwards 200–59
six-months old, child of 202–3
sleeping:
    broken 14–15, 226–33
    crying and 226, 227, 228–33
    new baby 176–7, 226, 227, 228–33
    pains during 121
    position 14
    room temperature and 14, 15
smell, sense of during pregnancy
        26, 34
socialising during pregnancy 40–2
solid food, feeding your baby on
        to 202, 236–40
stretch marks and veins 62–4
Strictly Come Dancing 14, 27, 30,
        42–7, 71, 123, 167, 188, 196–7
style:
    bra buying 66–7
    for little ones 254–5, 258
    shoes 67
    in the second trimester 65–7
    in the third trimester 98, 100
    waxing 102
    see also clothes
swimming 68
Syntocinon 145, 147
        ♡
taking your baby out and about
        for the first time 180–3

television escapism 33
temperature, room 14
tiredness/broken sleep 14–15,
        226–33
toys 252–3
travelling with children 204–9,
        215, 218–19
trimester:
    first: weeks 1 to 13 18–59
    second: weeks 14 to 27 60–87
    third: weeks 28 to due date
        88–127
        ♡
UK: Play 54
        ♡
vaccinations 224–5
Valetta, Amber 74
        ♡
waters breaking 13, 80–1
weaning 236–40
websites, list of useful 282–3
White Company 107, 113, 255
Wogan, Terry 28
work:
    in the first trimester 42–7
    in the second trimester 71–2
    in the third trimester 122
    returning to after birth 196–8,
        202, 278
        ♡
yoga 68

Acknowledgements

My first thank you goes to my mum and dad for being brilliant parents and the greatest role models. Only once you become a parent yourself do you suddenly realize 'hang on a minute, they're not *just* my mum and dad, they're actually saints!' My folks always gave me and my sister unconditional love and never once let us down (well, apart from the time, aged 11, when Mum refused to buy me that pair of to-die-for electric-blue lamé leggings from Littlewoods …). Anyway, I will always be grateful for a strong sense of family, strong roots and the self-esteem that goes with it. I just hope I can meet the same standards for my own children.

Thanks to my little girls for giving me the mad, all-consuming magic of motherhood. To Phoebe for lighting up our lives with her brilliant sense of fun and to Amber for her calm contented spirit and her ability to smile all day and sleep all night! To my sister Karen, my best friend who I miss every single day, who is an inspiringly brilliant mum to my gorgeous nephews Finn and Olly. To Gladys and Norman for being such loving grandparents and the best in-laws a girl could wish for (and for brewing up cups of tea on the hour when they come to visit).

Special thanks to Cherie and Paul for their love and kindness and to Anne. Major thanks are due to my obstetrician Claire Mellon who helped me believe I could deliver naturally when statistics gave me a 70 per cent chance. Thanks also to the very clever Peter Cass, and to Professor Morson who helped regulate my sometimes erratic hormones.

Thanks to my agent Polly and especially to Kat for all their help – I owe you big time. To Miranda for having the idea for the book in the first place and the faith to follow it through. To Anne-Marie for her help and guidance. Thanks for your patience while your own baby bump was growing by the day.

Lastly, but perhaps most importantly, thanks to my husband Vernon. Not only for being the best dad imaginable, but also for being the man that made me want to have babies in the first place. You rock!